HEDDA GABLER
and
A DOLL'S HOUSE

HEDDA GABLER

and

A DOLL'S HOUSE

HENRIK IBSEN

Translated by
CHRISTOPHER HAMPTON

faber and faber

LONDON · BOSTON

First published in 1989
by Faber and Faber Limited
3 Queen Square London WCIN 3AU

Photoset by Parker Typesetting Service Leicester
Printed in Great Britain by
Richard Clay Ltd Bungay Suffolk
All rights reserved

All rights whatsoever in these plays are strictly reserved and applications for
permission to perform them, etc., must be made in advance, before rehearsals
begin, to Margaret Ramsay Ltd, 14a Goodwin's Court, London WC2N 4LL.

A CIP record for this book
is available from the British Library

ISBN 0-571-14124-2

For Howard Davies

CONTENTS

HEDDA GABLER

CHARACTERS

HEDDA GABLER
GEORGE TESMAN
MISS TESMAN
BERTE
MRS ELVSTED
JUDGE BRACK
EILERT LOVBORG

The action takes place in Tesman's villa in the fashionable quarter of town.

ACT ONE   Morning
ACT TWO   Afternoon
ACT THREE   The next day at dawn
ACT FOUR   Evening

Christopher Hampton's adaptation of Henrik Ibsen's *Hedda Gabler*, from a literal translation by Hélène Grégoire, was first performed at the Stratford Festival Theatre, Ontario, on 10 June 1970.

The cast was as follows:

HEDDA GABLER	Irene Worth
GEORGE TESMAN	Gordon Jackson
MISS TESMAN	Anne Ives
BERTE	Christine Bennett
MRS ELVSTED	Gillian Martell
JUDGE BRACK	Donald Davis
EILERT LOVBORG	Leo Ciceri
Director	Peter Gill
Designer	Deirdre Clancy

It was revived at the Olivier Theatre, London, in February 1989 in a revised version from a literal translation by Karin and Ann Bamborough.

The cast was as follows:

HEDDA GABLER	Juliet Stevenson
GEORGE TESMAN	Paul Shelley
MISS TESMAN	Bridget Turner
BERTE	Janet Whiteside
MRS ELVSTED	Suzanne Burden
JUDGE BRACK	Norman Rodway
EILERT LOVBORG	Paul Jesson
Director	Howard Davies
Designer	Bob Crowley
Lighting	Mark Henderson

ACT ONE

*A spacious, attractive and tastefully furnished drawing room,
decorated in dark colours. At the back, a wide doorway, which leads,
as we can see through the open curtains, into a smaller room decorated
in the same style as the drawing room. In the right-hand wall of the
front room, a double door, which leads out into the hall, is partly
visible. In the opposite wall, on the left, a glass door, also with open
curtains. Through this door we can see a covered veranda and trees in
autumn colours. In the foreground, an oval table with a cover and a
number of chairs. Downstage, on the right-hand wall, a large dark
porcelain stove, a high-backed armchair, a footstool with a cushion
and two other stools. Upstage, in the right-hand corner, a sofa and
small round table. Another sofa downstage left, a little away from the
wall. Upstage of the glass door, a grand piano. Whatnots, with
terracotta and majolica ornaments, on either side of the doorway at the
back. Against the back wall of the inner room, a table and a couple of
chairs. Above the sofa, the portrait of a handsome, elderly man in a
general's uniform. Above the table, a hanging lamp with an opaque,
milk-white glass shade. Around the drawing room, a number of vases
and glasses with flowers in them. More flowers lying on the tables. The
floors in both rooms are thickly carpeted.*

Early morning. The sun streams in through the glass door. MISS
JULIANE TESMAN, *wearing a hat and carrying her parasol, comes in
from the hall, followed by* BERTE, *who carries a bunch of flowers
wrapped in paper.* MISS TESMAN *is about sixty-five; she looks pleasant
and kindly and is dressed neatly but simply in a grey outdoor suit.* BERTE,
the maid, is getting on in years; she looks plain and somewhat rustic.
MISS TESMAN *stops just inside the door, listens and speaks quietly.*

MISS TESMAN: My goodness, they must still be in bed.
BERTE: (*Also quietly*) That's what I was telling you, miss. You
    know how late the steamer got in last night. And then there
    was all that unpacking the young lady wanted done before
    she would go to bed, I don't know.

5

MISS TESMAN: Oh, well, let them have a good sleep. But they'll be glad of some nice fresh air when they do get up.
(*She goes over to the glass door and throws it wide open.*)

BERTE: (*By the table, not knowing where to put the flowers.*) There doesn't seem to be any room anywhere. I think I'll just leave them over here, miss.
(*She puts the flowers by the piano.*)

MISS TESMAN: Well, Berte dear, you've got a new mistress now. God knows, parting with you was almost more than I could bear.

BERTE: (*Close to tears*) What do you think it's like for me, miss? It's years and years I've been working for you.

MISS TESMAN: We'll have to make the best of it, Berte. There's nothing else we can do. George depends on you, you see: completely. After all, you have looked after him since he was a little boy.

BERTE: Yes, but I can't stop thinking about Miss Rina, miss. Lying at home there, absolutely helpless, poor thing. And that new maid. She'll never learn how to look after an invalid properly, never.

MISS TESMAN: Oh, it won't take me long to teach her. Anyway, I shall see to most of the work myself, you know that. You needn't worry about my poor sister, Berte dear.

BERTE: But that's not the only thing, miss. I'm so frightened Mrs Tesman will think I'm not suitable.

MISS TESMAN: Oh, well, there might be one or two things when you first start . . .

BERTE: She does seem a bit superior.

MISS TESMAN: Well, that's only to be expected. She is General Gabler's daughter. Think what sort of a life she must have had when the General was alive. Do you remember how she used to go out riding with her father? That long, black riding outfit? And the feather in her hat?

BERTE: Yes, oh yes, I do. But I never thought then she would finish up marrying our little student.

MISS TESMAN: No, I didn't either. Not that George is a student any more, Berte. From now on, you'll have to call him Dr Tesman.

BERTE: So Mrs Tesman was saying last night, soon as they set foot in the house. Is that really true, miss?

MISS TESMAN: Certainly. It's wonderful, isn't it, Berte? They made him a doctor when he was abroad, you know, on his tour. First thing I heard about it was when he told me last night on the quay.

BERTE: Well, I don't know, I'm sure he's clever enough to do anything. But I never thought he'd take up medicine.

MISS TESMAN: No, no, no, he's not that kind of doctor. (*Nods meaningfully.*) You might have to call him something even more important soon.

BERTE: And what might that be, miss?

MISS TESMAN: (*Smiling*) Aha, wouldn't you like to know? (*Moved.*) Oh, dear, oh, dear, if only poor Jochum could come back from the dead and see what's happened to his little boy. (*Looks around.*) Just a minute, Berte, what have you done? Why have you taken the loose covers off the furniture?

BERTE: Mrs Tesman said. She said she can't stand loose covers on the chairs.

MISS TESMAN: They're not going to use this room for everyday, are they?

BERTE: Yes, I think so. That's what Mrs Tesman said, anyway. He, er, the doctor, I mean, didn't open his mouth.

(GEORGE TESMAN *enters through the inner room, humming and carrying an empty, open suitcase. He is a young-looking man of average height, about thirty-three, quite plump, with a round, open, cheerful face and blond hair and beard. He wears glasses and comfortable, somewhat shabby indoor clothes.*)

MISS TESMAN: Good morning, George, good morning!

TESMAN: (*In the doorway*) Auntie Julia! (*Goes over to her and shakes her hand enthusiastically.*) Dear Auntie Julia. All this way. At this hour of the morning, mm?

MISS TESMAN: Well, I wanted to come and see how you were getting on.

TESMAN: But you can't have had a proper night's sleep.

MISS TESMAN: Oh, that doesn't matter at all.

7

TESMAN: Well. You . . . er . . . got home all right from the quay. Mm?

MISS TESMAN: Yes, quite all right, thank goodness. Judge Brack was kind enough to see me all the way to my door.

TESMAN: We were terribly sorry there wasn't room for you in our carriage. But you could see what a lot of luggage Hedda had with her, couldn't you?

MISS TESMAN: Yes, she certainly had a great deal of luggage.

BERTE: (*To* TESMAN) Shall I go and ask Mrs Tesman if there's anything I can do to help?

TESMAN: No, thank you, Berte, never mind. She said she'd ring if she wanted anything.

BERTE: (*Moving towards the right*) All right, then.

TESMAN: One thing, look, could you just put this suitcase away somewhere?

BERTE: (*Taking it*) I'll put it in the attic.
(*She goes out through the hall door.*)

TESMAN: Can you imagine, Auntie, that suitcase was absolutely bursting with copies I made of various documents. All those archives I looked at, I made the most incredible discoveries. Strange forgotten details nobody else knows anything about.

MISS TESMAN: Well, you don't seem to have wasted any time on your honeymoon, George.

TESMAN: No, I haven't, no, no. Why don't you take your bonnet off, Auntie? May I undo the bow, mm?

MISS TESMAN: (*As he does so*) Dear, oh, dear, it's just as if you'd never left home.

TESMAN: (*Turning the hat around in his hand*) What a lovely smart hat you've bought yourself.

MISS TESMAN: I bought it because of Hedda.

TESMAN: Mm? Because of Hedda?

MISS TESMAN: Yes, so Hedda wouldn't be ashamed of me if we went out for a walk.

TESMAN: (*Stroking her cheek*) Really, you think of everything, Auntie Julia. (*Puts the hat down on a chair by the table.*) Now. Look. Why don't we sit down on the sofa and have a little chat before Hedda joins us?

8

6/10/93

(*They sit down. She puts her parasol in a corner on the sofa.*)

MISS TESMAN: (*Taking both his hands and looking at him*) It's marvellous to see you again, George, sitting there large as life. Poor Jochum's little boy.

TESMAN: And for me, Auntie Julia, to see you. I mean, to me, you've always seemed like a mother and a father.

MISS TESMAN: Yes, I'm sure you'll go on being fond of your old aunt.

TESMAN: And how's Auntie Rina? Is there any improvement, mm?

MISS TESMAN: Oh, no, poor thing, I don't think we can hope for any improvement. There she is, lying there just as helpless as she has been all these years. I only hope God lets me keep her for a little bit longer. Otherwise, I wouldn't know what to do with my life, George. Especially now I don't have you to look after any more.

TESMAN: (*Patting her on the back*) Now then, there, there.

MISS TESMAN: (*A sudden change of tone*) I can't get over the fact that you're married now, George. And to Hedda Gabler of all people, the beautiful Hedda Gabler. It's extraordinary, when you think of how many admirers she used to have.

TESMAN: (*Humming a little and smiling, complacently*) Yes, I should think quite a few of my friends in town must be pretty jealous, don't you think, mm?

MISS TESMAN: And you had such a lovely long honeymoon – five, no more than that, nearly six months.

TESMAN: Well, I did have a lot of research to do. Investigating all those archives and ploughing through mountains of books.

MISS TESMAN: Yes, I know you did. (*Lowers her voice confidentially.*) Listen, George, you haven't, you haven't anything special to tell me, have you?

TESMAN: About the tour?

MISS TESMAN: Yes.

TESMAN: No, I don't think there was anything except what I told you in my letters. I took my doctor's degree abroad, but I told you about that yesterday.

MISS TESMAN: Yes, yes, I know about that. What I meant was I was wondering if you had any . . . expectations.

TESMAN: Expectations?

MISS TESMAN: Oh, George, I am your auntie after all.

TESMAN: Well, of course I've got expectations.

MISS TESMAN: You have?

TESMAN: Yes, I expect to be made a professor before very long. That's my main expectation.

MISS TESMAN: Yes, to be made a professor, but . . .

TESMAN: Yes, I might even say it's a certainty. But, Auntie, you know about that already, dear.

MISS TESMAN: (*Chuckling*) Yes, you're right, I do, yes. (*Changes the subject.*) But your tour must have cost an awful lot of money, George.

TESMAN: Yes, well, the grant was very generous, that went quite a long way towards it.

MISS TESMAN: Yes, but what I can't understand is how you stretched it out to pay for both of you.

TESMAN: Ah, that is rather extraordinary, isn't it, mm?

MISS TESMAN: Not only that, but they always say travelling with a lady is inordinately expensive.

TESMAN: Yes, that's to be expected, it does mean a little extra expense. But Hedda had to have that trip, Auntie. Really, she had to. Nothing else would have done.

MISS TESMAN: No, I suppose not. People always seem to insist on a honeymoon abroad nowadays. Now, what I want to know is whether you've had a proper look round the house yet.

TESMAN: Oh, yes, I've been up and about since dawn.

MISS TESMAN: And what do you think of it?

TESMAN: It's marvellous. Absolutely marvellous. The only thing I'm not sure about is what we're going to do with those two empty rooms between the back room there and Hedda's bedroom.

MISS TESMAN: (*Chuckling*) Ah, George, dear, I expect you'll find some use for them, sooner or later.

TESMAN: Yes, Auntie, I'm sure you're right. Somewhere to put all those extra books.

MISS TESMAN: Yes, dear, books, yes, that's what I meant.

TESMAN: Anyway, it's because of Hedda that I'm really pleased about the house. Before we were engaged, she always used to say the only place she really wanted to live was Secretary Falk's villa.

MISS TESMAN: Amazing that it should have come up for sale just after you went away.

TESMAN: Yes, Auntie, the luck's really been on our side, hasn't it, mm?

MISS TESMAN: But it's expensive, isn't it, George? It's all going to be very expensive.

TESMAN: (*Somewhat crestfallen*) Yes, I suppose it is.

MISS TESMAN: Of course it is.

TESMAN: How much would you say? I mean approximately? Mm?

MISS TESMAN: Won't be able to tell until I see all the bills.

TESMAN: Well, luckily Judge Brack has managed to get me the very best terms. He wrote to Hedda about it.

MISS TESMAN: There's no need to worry about it, dear. I've given a guarantee for the furniture and all the carpets.

TESMAN: Guarantee? You have? But how could you, Auntie? What kind of guarantee?

MISS TESMAN: I've taken out a mortgage on our annuity.

TESMAN: (*Jumping to his feet*) What? You mean on the annuity you and Auntie Rina . . .

MISS TESMAN: Well, I couldn't think what else to do.

TESMAN: (*Standing in front of her*) But, Auntie, have you gone mad? Mm? That annuity is the only thing you and Auntie Rina have to live on.

MISS TESMAN: Now, don't upset yourself. It's only a formality, you know. That's what Judge Brack said. He was kind enough to make all the arrangements for me. And he said it was only a formality.

TESMAN: Yes, that's as may be. All the same . . .

MISS TESMAN: Anyway, from now on you'll have your salary coming in. And, good Lord, what if it does cost us a bit? A little something to start you off with, you know we'd be only too pleased.

TESMAN: Oh, Auntie, you're always ready to make sacrifices for me.

MISS TESMAN: (*Getting up and putting her hand on his shoulder*) My dear boy, what other pleasures do I have in this world, besides helping to smooth your way? After all, you've had no father or mother to turn to. And we've got what we were aiming for now. Sometimes things have seemed very black. But, thank God, George, you've come through it all.

TESMAN: Yes, strange, isn't it, how everything has worked out for the best?

MISS TESMAN: Yes, and the people who stood in your way and tried to hold you back have come to grief, George, and fallen by the wayside. The biggest threat of all is the one who fell the hardest. And as he made his bed, so he must lie on it, poor misguided wretch.

TESMAN: Have you had any more news about Eilert? Since I went away, I mean?

MISS TESMAN: No. Except he's supposed to have published some new book.

TESMAN: Really? What, Eilert Lovborg? Recent, is that, mm?

MISS TESMAN: Yes, apparently. Goodness knows whether it's any good. Now when your new book comes out, George, that'll be a different matter. What's it about?

TESMAN: Medieval husbandry in Brabant.

MISS TESMAN: Fancy you being able to write about that sort of thing!

TESMAN: Mind you, it'll probably be some time before it comes out. I've got all those papers to sort through and catalogue first, you see.

MISS TESMAN: Yes, sorting and cataloguing, you know all about that. You're Jochum's son, all right.

TESMAN: Anyway, I'm certainly looking forward to getting down to work. Especially now I've got my own home sweet home to work in.

MISS TESMAN: And now you've got the wife you set your heart on, George dear, that's the most important thing of all.

TESMAN: (*Putting his arms round her*) Oh, yes, Auntie, yes. Hedda. She's the most wonderful thing that ever happened to me. (*Looks over to the doorway.*) That's her now, isn't it, mm?

(HEDDA *enters from the left through the back room. She is a woman of twenty-nine. Her face and figure are refined and distinguished. Her complexion is pale and lustreless. Her eyes are steel-grey, cold, clear and calm. Her medium brown hair is beautiful, without being particularly abundant. She wears a tasteful, loose-fitting morning gown.*)

MISS TESMAN: (*Going to meet* HEDDA) Good morning, Hedda, my dear. How are you, good morning.

HEDDA: Good morning, Miss Tesman. How kind of you to call. And so early.

MISS TESMAN: (*Somewhat embarrassed*) Well, and . . . er . . . did the bride sleep well in her new home?

HEDDA: Yes, thank you. Tolerably.

TESMAN: (*Laughing*) Tolerably? Come on, Hedda, you were sleeping like a log when I got up.

HEDDA: Fortunately. It always takes time to get used to anything new, Miss Tesman. It's a gradual business. (*Looks over to the left.*) Ah, the maid's left the veranda door open, all that sun pouring in.

MISS TESMAN: (*Moving towards the door*) Well, let's shut it, then.

HEDDA: No, no, don't. Tesman, draw the curtain. Give us a softer light.

TESMAN: (*At the door*) Of course. There we are, Hedda, shade *and* fresh air.

HEDDA: Yes, we could do with some fresh air. All these wretched flowers. Now, won't you sit down, Miss Tesman?

MISS TESMAN: No, thank you. Now I know everything's all right here, I'd better be getting along home. My sister will be lying waiting, she misses me very badly when I'm away, poor dear.

TESMAN: Don't forget to give her my love. And tell her I'll be popping in to see her later on in the day.

MISS TESMAN: Yes, all right, I will, Oh, by the way, George . . . (*Fumbles in the pocket of her dress.*) I almost forgot, I've got something for you.

TESMAN: What? What is it, Auntie? Mm?

MISS TESMAN: (*Pulling out a flat parcel wrapped in newspaper and handing it to him*) Here you are, dear.

TESMAN: (*Opening it*) Ah, Auntie Julia, no, did you save them for me? Hedda! Isn't that really touching, don't you think, mm?

HEDDA: (*Beside the whatnot on the right*) Yes, dear. What is it?

TESMAN: My old house shoes. You know, my slippers.

HEDDA: Oh, yes, I remember you talked about them frequently while we were abroad.

TESMAN: Well, I missed them so much. (*Goes over to her.*) Here they are, Hedda, have a look.

HEDDA: (*Crossing to the stove*) No, thanks, I'd really rather not.

TESMAN: (*Following her*) Can you imagine, Auntie Rina embroidered them for me herself, even though she was ill in bed. You can't think how many memories they bring back.

HEDDA: (*By the table*) Not to me.

MISS TESMAN: Hedda has a point there, George.

TESMAN: Yes, but I mean, now she's one of the family . . .

HEDDA: (*Interrupting*) We'll never be able to put up with that maid, Tesman.

MISS TESMAN: With Berte?

TESMAN: Whatever makes you think that, dear? Mm?

HEDDA: (*Pointing*) Well, she's left her old hat on the chair, look.

TESMAN: (*Dropping his slippers on the floor in amazement*) But, Hedda . . .

HEDDA: Anyone could come in and see it.

TESMAN: But, Hedda, that's Auntie Julia's bonnet.

HEDDA: Oh, really?

MISS TESMAN: (*Picking up the hat*) Yes, it is mine. And it's not old either, Hedda.

HEDDA: I really didn't look at it very carefully, Miss Tesman.

MISS TESMAN: (*Trying the hat on*) It's actually the first time I've ever worn it, I can assure you of that.

TESMAN: Well, and very nice it is too. Beautiful.

MISS TESMAN: No, George, it's very ordinary. (*Looks around her.*) Now, where's that parasol? Ah. (*Picks it up.*) That's mine as well. (*Mumbles*) Not Berte's.

TESMAN: A new hat and a new parasol, can you imagine, Hedda?

HEDDA: Yes, very pretty, lovely.

TESMAN: Yes, they are, aren't they? Mm? Auntie, before you go

have a good look at Hedda. Now she is very pretty and
lovely.

MISS TESMAN: Well, my dear, there's nothing surprising about
that. Hedda's been beautiful all her life.
(*She nods and moves towards the right.*)

TESMAN: (*Following*) Yes, but have you noticed how chubby and
healthy she looks? She really filled out while we were abroad.

HEDDA: (*Crossing the room*) Oh, that's enough!

MISS TESMAN: (*Stops and turns round*) Filled out?

TESMAN: Yes, Auntie, it doesn't show very much when she's got
that dress on. But I'm lucky enough . . .

HEDDA: (*By the glass door, impatiently*) You're not lucky enough
for anything.

TESMAN: It's probably the mountain air in the Tyrol . . .

HEDDA: (*Interrupting curtly*) I'm exactly the same now as I was
when I went away.

TESMAN: So you keep saying. But you're not. Don't you agree
with me, Auntie?

MISS TESMAN: (*Stands looking at her with folded hands*) Hedda is
beautiful, beautiful, beautiful. (*Goes up to her, takes her head
in both hands, bends it forward and kisses her hair.*) God bless
you and keep you, Hedda Tesman. For George's sake.

HEDDA: (*Gently freeing herself*) Oh . . . let go of me.

MISS TESMAN: (*Quietly moved*) I shall come and see you both
every day.

TESMAN: Yes, Auntie, you make sure you do, mm?

MISS TESMAN: Goodbye, goodbye.
(*She goes out through the hall door.* TESMAN *follows her,
leaving the door ajar. We hear* TESMAN *repeating his good
wishes to Auntie Rina and his thanks for the slippers.
Meanwhile,* HEDDA *walks across the room and raises her arms,
clenching her hands as if in anger. She draws the curtains in front
of the glass door and stands there, looking out. A moment later,*
TESMAN *reappears, closing the door behind him.*)

TESMAN: (*Picking up his slippers from the floor*) What are you
looking at, Hedda?

HEDDA: (*Calm and controlled now*) I'm just standing here looking at the leaves. They're so yellow. And dried up.

TESMAN: (*Wrapping up the slippers and putting them down on the table*) Yes, we're well into September now, after all.

HEDDA: (*Restless again*) Yes, we are. Already in . . . into September.

TESMAN: Didn't you think Auntie Julia was a bit odd today? Sort of formal? Any idea what was the matter with her? Mm?

HEDDA: I hardly know her. Isn't she usually like that?

TESMAN: No, not as a rule.

HEDDA: (*Moving away from the glass door*) Was she upset by what I said about her hat, do you think?

TESMAN: Oh, not particularly. Perhaps at the time she was a little.

HEDDA: But fancy leaving your hat lying around like that in the drawing room. It's just not done.

TESMAN: Well, I'm sure Auntie Julia won't do it again.

HEDDA: Anyway, I shall try to make it up with her.

TESMAN: Yes, Hedda, if you could, dear, that would be nice.

HEDDA: When you go and see them this afternoon, why don't you ask her for the evening?

TESMAN: Yes, I will, I will. And there's one other thing you could do that would really make her happy.

HEDDA: What?

TESMAN: If you could perhaps stop calling her Miss Tesman, mm? For my sake.

HEDDA: No, Tesman, I couldn't. You mustn't keep asking me, we've discussed this before. If you like I'll try to call her Aunt, all right? But that's the best I can do.

TESMAN: It's just that now you're one of the family . . .

HEDDA: I can't see what . . .

(*She crosses over to the door.*)

TESMAN: (*After a pause*) Is anything the matter? Mm?

HEDDA: I'm just looking at my old piano. It doesn't go very well with all the other things.

TESMAN: Well, as soon as I start getting my salary, we'll see about having it exchanged.

HEDDA: Exchanged? That's not what I meant, I don't want to get rid of it. I thought we could move it into the back room there, and get another one to put here in its place. I mean, as soon as we can manage it.

TESMAN: (*Slightly dejected*) Oh. Yes, well, why not?

HEDDA: (*Picking the bouquet up from the piano*) These flowers weren't here when we got in last night.

TESMAN: Auntie Julia probably brought them for you.

HEDDA: (*Examining the bouquet*) Here's a visiting card. (*Takes it out and reads it.*) 'Will call in again later on today.' Guess who it's from?

TESMAN: I don't know. Who? Mm?

HEDDA: It says 'Mrs Elvsted'.

TESMAN: Really? Wasn't she Miss Rysing? Before she married the magistrate?

HEDDA: Yes, that's right. She had that irritating hair she was always flaunting. I was told she was an old flame of yours.

TESMAN: (*Laughing*) Oh, that didn't last long. And it was before I met you, Hedda. But what's she doing in town? It's extraordinary.

HEDDA: It's strange she should want to call on us. I haven't seen her since I left school.

TESMAN: Yes, it's God knows how long since I've seen her. I don't know how she puts up with it, living up there in that out-of-the-way hole, do you? Mm?

HEDDA: (*Considers a moment and then says suddenly*) Listen, Tesman, doesn't he . . . live somewhere up round there? . . . Eilert Lovborg?

TESMAN: Yes, somewhere in that area.

(BERTE *appears in the hall doorway.*)

BERTE: That lady who called a while ago and left some flowers is here again, madam. (*Points to the flowers.*) Those flowers you're holding.

HEDDA: Oh, is she? Would you show her in, please?

(BERTE *opens the door for* MRS ELVSTED *and goes out herself.* MRS ELVSTED *is a fragile-looking woman with beautiful, soft features. Her eyes are pale blue, large, round and somewhat protruding, with a frightened and puzzled expression. Her hair is*

*remarkably fair, almost flaxen, abundant and wavy. She is a
few years younger than* HEDDA. *She wears a dark morning suit,
tasteful, but not quite in the latest fashion.*)

(*Approaching her warmly*) How are you, Mrs Elvsted? It's
lovely to see you again.

MRS ELVSTED: (*Trying to control her nervousness*) Well, it's been a
very long time . . .

TESMAN: (*Stretching out his hand*) Yes, it has, hasn't it? Mm?

HEDDA: Thank you for the beautiful flowers.

MRS ELVSTED: Oh, that's all right . . . I wanted to come straight
here yesterday afternoon, but I heard you were still away . . .

TESMAN: You've only just arrived in town, have you? Mm?

MRS ELVSTED: Yesterday afternoon. I got quite desperate when I
heard you weren't at home.

HEDDA: Desperate? Why?

TESMAN: But, my dear Mrs Rysing . . . I mean, Mrs Elvsted . . .

HEDDA: I hope there's nothing wrong.

MRS ELVSTED: Yes, there is. And I don't know a single person
here I can turn to, except for you.

HEDDA: (*Putting the bouquet down on the table*) Come on, let's sit
down here on the sofa.

MRS ELVSTED: Oh, I feel much too restless to sit down.

HEDDA: No, you don't. Come on.

(*She pushes* MRS ELVSTED *down on the sofa and sits next to
her.*)

TESMAN: Now, what's the matter, Mrs erm . . .?

HEDDA: Is there something wrong at home?

MRS ELVSTED: Yes, well, there is and there isn't. The thing is, I
don't want you to misunderstand me.

HEDDA: Well then, you'd better tell us everything as plainly as
possible.

TESMAN: After all, I expect that's why you came, isn't it, mm?

MRS ELVSTED: Yes, of course it is . . . well . . . I should tell you,
if you don't already know, that Eilert Lovborg is here in
town.

HEDDA: Lovborg . . .

TESMAN: No, really, has Eilert Lovborg come back? Did you

hear that, Hedda? Extraordinary!

HEDDA: Of course I heard, my God.

MRS ELVSTED: He's been here about a week already. A whole week. In this dangerous town. Alone! Mixing in all that bad company.

HEDDA: But, my dear Mrs Elvsted, what's he got to do with you?

MRS ELVSTED: (*Frightened, she looks up at* HEDDA *and speaks quickly*) Oh, well, he used to be the children's tutor.

HEDDA: You have children?

MRS ELVSTED: No, no, I don't. They're my husband's.

HEDDA: Oh, your stepchildren.

MRS ELVSTED: Yes.

TESMAN: (*Groping for the words*) But was he sufficiently . . . er . . . I don't quite know how to put this . . . was he, um, sufficiently regular in his way of life to be suitable for a job like that? Mm?

MRS ELVSTED: In the last two years his behaviour has been impeccable.

TESMAN: Really? Extraordinary. Did you hear that, Hedda?

HEDDA: Yes, I did.

MRS ELVSTED: Impeccable. I promise you. In every way. But even so, now I know he's here in a big town, with all that money on him . . . I'm terrified of what might happen to him.

TESMAN: But why didn't he stay where he was? With you and your husband? Mm?

MRS ELVSTED: Since his book was published, he's been far too restless to settle down at home.

TESMAN: Yes, that's right. Auntie Julia told me he'd published a new book.

MRS ELVSTED: Yes, it's a wonderful new book about the history of civilization, sort of a general outline. It's been out about a fortnight. It's sold very well, a lot of people have read it, it's caused something of a sensation . . .

TESMAN: Has it? I suppose it must be something he's been saving since . . . happier days.

MRS ELVSTED: Do you mean some time ago?

TESMAN: Yes.

MRS ELVSTED: Oh, no, he's written it all since he came to us . . . over the last year.

TESMAN: Well, that's good tidings, isn't it, Hedda? Extraordinary.

MRS ELVSTED: Yes, if only it would last.

HEDDA: Have you found him yet?

MRS ELVSTED: No, not yet. I had the greatest difficulty tracking down his address. But I finally managed to this morning.

HEDDA: (*Looking inquiringly at her*) Actually, I think it's a bit strange that your husband . . . ah . . .

MRS ELVSTED: (*Starting nervously*) My husband? What do you mean?

HEDDA: Well, that he should send you into town to run his errands. And not come in himself to look after his friend.

MRS ELVSTED: Oh, no, my husband hasn't the time for that kind of thing. Anyway, I had some shopping to do.

HEDDA: (*Ghost of a smile*) Oh, well, then . . .

MRS ELVSTED: (*Getting up hastily and rather uneasily*) I just wanted to ask you, Mr Tesman, please be kind to Eilert Lovborg if he comes to see you, please. Because I'm sure he will. After all, you used to be very close friends. And aren't you both studying the same subject? You're in the same faculty, aren't you? As far as I can remember.

TESMAN: Used to be, anyway, yes.

MRS ELVSTED: Well then, please, can I ask you very seriously to keep a sharp eye on him, as well? Will you promise me that, Mr Tesman, will you?

TESMAN: Of course, it'll be a pleasure, Mrs Rysing . . .

HEDDA: Elvsted.

TESMAN: I'll do anything I can for Eilert, I promise. You can rely on me.

MRS ELVSTED: That's terribly kind of you. (*Presses his hands.*) Thank you, thank you, thank you. (*Frightened.*) It's my husband, you see, he thinks such a lot of him.

HEDDA: (*Getting up*) You ought to write to him, Tesman. He might not come to see you of his own accord.

TESMAN: Yes, Hedda, perhaps that might be the best way of going about things, do you think? Mm?

HEDDA: The sooner the better. Now, I'd say.

MRS ELVSTED: (*Imploringly*) Oh, why don't you?

TESMAN: I'll write to him now, Mrs erm, this minute. Have you got his address, Mrs . . . Elvsted?

MRS ELVSTED: Yes. (*Takes a small piece of paper out of her pocket and gives it to him.*) Here.

TESMAN: Good, well done. I'll go and do it now then. (*Casts about him.*) Just a minute. Where are my slippers? Oh, yes. (*He picks up the packet and is on his way out.*)

HEDDA: Make it a warm, friendly letter, will you? And long.

TESMAN: Right.

MRS ELVSTED: But don't tell him I asked you, please, will you?

TESMAN: Of course not, that goes without saying, doesn't it? Mm?

(*He exits through the back room.*)

HEDDA: (*Going over to* MRS ELVSTED, *smiling and speaking in a low voice*) That is killing two birds with one stone.

MRS ELVSTED: What do you mean?

HEDDA: Couldn't you tell I was trying to get rid of him?

MRS ELVSTED: Well, yes, to write the letter . . .

HEDDA: And because I wanted to talk to you alone.

MRS ELVSTED: (*Confused*) About the same thing?

HEDDA: Exactly.

MRS ELVSTED: (*Apprehensively*) But there's nothing more to say about it, Mrs Tesman. Honestly, nothing.

HEDDA: Oh, yes, there is. A lot. I can tell. Come here. Come and sit down and we can have a nice, private conversation. (*She forces* MRS ELVSTED *to sit in the armchair by the stove and then sits on one of the stools.*)

MRS ELVSTED: (*Looking nervously at her watch*) But, Mrs Tesman, I really think it's time I was on my way.

HEDDA: I'm sure you can't be in that much of a hurry. Now. Tell me something about what sort of life you lead at home.

MRS ELVSTED: That's the last thing I want to talk about.

HEDDA: Even to me? After all, dear, we were at school together.

MRS ELVSTED: Yes, but you were in the class above me. And I was terribly frightened of you in those days.

HEDDA: Frightened? Of me?

MRS ELVSTED: Yes. Terribly frightened. When we passed on the stairs you always used to pull my hair.

HEDDA: I didn't, did I?

MRS ELVSTED: Yes, and one day you said you wanted to set fire to it.

HEDDA: Yes, but that was just fooling about, you must know that.

MRS ELVSTED: Yes, but I was so stupid in those days. And since then, I mean since we left school, we seem to have drifted such a long . . . such a long way away from each other. We've moved in completely different circles.

HEDDA: Well, now's our chance to get together again. Listen, we used to be very friendly at school. We used to call each other by our Christian names.

MRS ELVSTED: I don't think so. I think you must be mistaken.

HEDDA: Of course I'm not. No, I remember distinctly. So let's be friends now, as we were in the old days. (*Moves the stool nearer to* MRS ELVSTED.) All right? (*Kisses her on the cheek.*) And you must call me Hedda.

MRS ELVSTED: (*Pressing and stroking her hands*) You're very kind to me. I'm not really used to kindness.

HEDDA: It's all right. I'll be your friend again, as I was before, and call you Thora.

MRS ELVSTED: Thea it is, actually.

HEDDA: Thea, yes, that's right. Of course. That's what I meant. (*Looks at her sympathetically.*) So, Thea, you're not really used to kindness? Not even in your own home?

MRS ELVSTED: Well, perhaps if I had a home. But I haven't. I never have had.

HEDDA: (*Considers her for a moment*) I thought it might be something like that.

MRS ELVSTED: (*Looking helplessly in front of her*) Yes . . . yes . . . yes.

HEDDA: I can't quite remember. But when you first went up to

22

the magistrate's house, didn't you go as housekeeper?

MRS ELVSTED: No, governess they took me on as in the first place. But his wife, I mean his first wife, wasn't very well. She was bedridden most of the time. So I had to look after the house as well.

HEDDA: Until in the end it was your house.

MRS ELVSTED: (*Sadly*) Yes, that's right.

HEDDA: Now, let me think. How long is it since you . . .?

MRS ELVSTED: Since I got married?

HEDDA: Yes.

MRS ELVSTED: Five years.

HEDDA: Yes, that's right, it must be.

MRS ELVSTED: Those five years! Especially the last two or three of them. You can't imagine what it's been like, Mrs Tesman.

HEDDA: (*Tapping her lightly on the hand*) Mrs Tesman? Now really, Thea.

MRS ELVSTED: Yes, I'm sorry. I'll try . . . Hedda. You can't begin to imagine what it's been like . . .

HEDDA: (*Casually*) Eilert Lovborg's been up with you for about three years, hasn't he?

MRS ELVSTED: (*Looking at her dubiously*) Eilert Lovborg? Yes.

HEDDA: Did you know him before, when you were living here?

MRS ELVSTED: Not really. I mean, I'd heard of him, obviously.

HEDDA: But when he moved to the country, you saw quite a lot of him?

MRS ELVSTED: Yes, he used to come every day. To give the children lessons. In the end I found I couldn't manage everything on my own.

HEDDA: No, I can understand that. What about your husband? Does he have to do a lot of travelling?

MRS ELVSTED: Yes. As a magistrate, he has to travel about quite a bit in his district, well, I'm sure you know that, Mrs . . . er, Hedda.

HEDDA: (*Leaning against the arm of the chair*) Poor Thea. Listen, Thea, dear, you're going to tell me everything now, the whole story.

MRS ELVSTED: It's better if you ask the questions.

HEDDA: What kind of man is your husband, Thea? I mean, you know, what's he like at home? Is he good to you?

MRS ELVSTED: (*Evasively*) Well, I think he believes that everything he does is for the best.

HEDDA: It's just I was thinking he's probably rather old for you. More than twenty years older, isn't he?

MRS ELVSTED: (*Irritably*) Yes, there's that as well. And there are other things. Everything about him disgusts me! I mean, we have nothing in common, neither of us, not a single thought.

HEDDA: But he cares for you, doesn't he? In his own way?

MRS ELVSTED: Oh, I don't know what he feels. I'm useful to him anyway, and that's probably as far as it goes. And I don't cost him very much either. I'm very cheap.

HEDDA: That's very silly of you.

MRS ELVSTED: (*Shaking her head*) It'll never change. Not with him. I don't think he cares for anyone but himself. Except the children, perhaps.

HEDDA: And Eilert Lovborg.

MRS ELVSTED: (*Looking at her*) Eilert Lovborg? What makes you think that?

HEDDA: Well, if he sends you all this way into town to look for him. (*An almost imperceptible smile.*) Anyway, that's what you said to Tesman.

MRS ELVSTED: (*A nervous twitch*) Was it? Yes, I suppose it was. (*Quietly, but vehemently*) I might just as well tell you everything. It's bound to come out sooner or later anyway.

HEDDA: What is, Thea?

MRS ELVSTED: Well, to cut a long story short, my husband didn't know I was coming.

HEDDA: What? Didn't he know anything about it?

MRS ELVSTED: Of course he didn't. He wasn't even at home. He's away, travelling. I just couldn't stand it any longer, Hedda! I really couldn't. Spending the rest of my life up there completely on my own.

HEDDA: So . . .?

MRS ELVSTED: So I packed a few of my things. What I needed most. As discreetly as I could. And left the house.

HEDDA: Without telling anyone?

MRS ELVSTED: Yes, and I caught the train into town.

HEDDA: But, Thea, my dear, I don't know how you dared.

MRS ELVSTED: (*Getting up and crossing the room*) What else could I have done?

HEDDA: But what's your husband going to say when you get back?

MRS ELVSTED: (*By the table, looking across at her*) Back to him?

HEDDA: Well, yes.

MRS ELVSTED: I'm not going back to him. Ever.

HEDDA: (*Getting up and moving towards her*) You mean . . . you've left home now . . . for good?

MRS ELVSTED: Yes. There didn't seem to be any alternative.

HEDDA: What, openly? Just like that?

MRS ELVSTED: Well, you can't very well keep a thing like that secret, can you?

HEDDA: But, Thea, what do you think people are going to say about all this?

MRS ELVSTED: I don't know, they can say what they like. (*Sits down sadly and wearily on the sofa.*) What I've done, I did because I had to.

HEDDA: (*After a short silence*) And what are you thinking of doing now? How will you proceed?

MRS ELVSTED: I don't know. All I know is, I must live here, where Eilert Lovborg is, if I'm to live at all.

HEDDA: (*Moving a chair from the table, sitting next to her and stroking her hands*) Thea, tell me, how did this . . . friendship develop between you and Eilert Lovborg?

MRS ELVSTED: Oh, it happened gradually. And after a bit I found I had a kind of power over him.

HEDDA: Oh, really?

MRS ELVSTED: And he started giving up his old habits. Not that I asked him to, I'd never have dared to do that. But I'm sure he noticed how much they upset me. So he just abandoned them.

HEDDA: (*Concealing an involuntary smile of contempt*) So, little Thea to the rescue, you might say.

MRS ELVSTED: Well, that's what he says, anyway. And in return he . . . showed me how to be a real human being. Taught me how to think, and how to understand all sorts of things.

HEDDA: So he gave you lessons as well, did he?

MRS ELVSTED: Well, not exactly lessons. He just talked to me. We talked endlessly about everything. And then there was a wonderfully happy time when he let me share in his work. And help him.

HEDDA: He let you do that?

MRS ELVSTED: Oh, yes! Whenever he wrote anything, we always worked at it together.

HEDDA: Soul mates, were you?

MRS ELVSTED: (*Enthusiastically*) Soul mates! It's funny, Hedda, that's what he used to say. I ought to feel gloriously happy. But I can't, because I don't know how long it's going to last.

HEDDA: Don't you trust him any more than that?

MRS ELVSTED: (*Sadly*) There's still something between Eilert Lovborg and me. The shadow of a woman.

HEDDA: (*Looking at her in suspense*) Who?

MRS ELVSTED: I don't know. Someone in his . . . in the past. Someone he's never quite been able to forget.

HEDDA: What has he told you about her?

MRS ELVSTED: He's only ever made one casual reference to her.

HEDDA: And what did he say?

MRS ELVSTED: He said that when they had to part, she threatened to shoot him with her pistol.

HEDDA: (*Cold, composed*) Oh, nonsense, people never behave like that.

MRS ELVSTED: No. That's why I think it must be that red-headed singer he used to . . .

HEDDA: Yes, very probably.

MRS ELVSTED: I remember hearing about her; apparently she used to carry loaded guns.

HEDDA: Oh, well then, it must have been her.

MRS ELVSTED: (*Wringing her hands*) Yes, but the thing is, Hedda, I've just heard that the singer is here in town. Oh, I feel so desperate . . .

HEDDA: (*Glancing towards the back room*) Sh! Here's Tesman. (*Gets up and whispers.*) Thea, all this is between you and me.

MRS ELVSTED: (*Jumping up*) Oh, yes, please, for God's sake . . .
(GEORGE TESMAN *comes in from the right, through the back room, holding a letter.*)

TESMAN: Well, here's my missive. All signed and sealed.

HEDDA: Good. I think Mrs Elvsted has to be going now. Wait a minute, I'll just see her to the garden gate.

TESMAN: Hedda, perhaps Berte could take care of this, could she?

HEDDA: (*Taking the letter*) Yes, I'll tell her.
(BERTE *comes into the front room.*)

BERTE: Judge Brack is here. He says he'd like to see you.

HEDDA: Yes, show him in, would you? And listen, could you put this letter in the post?

BERTE: (*Taking the letter*) Yes, madam.
(*She opens the door for* JUDGE BRACK, *and then goes out. The judge is a man of about forty-five – thickset, but well built and supple in his movements. A roundish face with a distinguished profile. His hair is cut short, still almost black and meticulously groomed. His eyes are lively and alert. His eyebrows are luxuriant, as is his moustache, with the ends clipped short. He wears an elegant walking suit, which is a little too young for him. He uses a monocle, which now and then he lets drop.*)

BRACK: (*Hat in hand, bowing*) You don't mind my calling so early in the day?

HEDDA: Not in the least.

TESMAN: (*Shaking his hand*) You're always welcome. (*Introducing him*) Judge Brack, Miss Rysing . . .

HEDDA: Oh . . .

BRACK: (*Bowing*) Pleased to meet you.

HEDDA: (*Looking at him and smiling*) I'm not used to seeing you in daylight, Judge.

BRACK: Do I look different?

HEDDA: A little younger, I think.

BRACK: Thank you kindly.

TESMAN: And what about Hedda, mm? Doesn't she look healthy? She's actually . . .

HEDDA: Oh, don't keep on about me. You'd do better to thank Judge Brack for all the trouble he's taken.

BRACK: But that was my pleasure.

HEDDA: You're very devoted. Look, my friend here's dying to get away. I'll see you in a minute, Judge. I won't be long. (*General salutations.* MRS ELVSTED *and* HEDDA *go out through the hall door.*)

BRACK: Well, is your wife reasonably pleased?

TESMAN: Yes, we can't thank you enough. I mean, she tells me there are still one or two changes she wants made. And a few things she still needs. So I expect we shall have to make a few more minor purchases.

BRACK: Oh? Really?

TESMAN: But we're not going to bother you any more. Hedda said that what she needed she would see to herself. Let's sit down, shall we, mm?

BRACK: Thank you, just for a minute. (*Sits down by the table.*) There's something I wanted to talk to you about, Tesman.

TESMAN: Is there? Oh, I know. (*Sits down.*) I suppose it's time for the after-dinner speeches now, is it, fundamentals, mm?

BRACK: You mean the financial arrangements, oh, no, there's nothing very pressing about them. Although I am beginning to wish we'd set about things a little more modestly.

TESMAN: But how could we have done? What about Hedda? You know her well enough by now, don't you? You know I couldn't possibly expect her to put up with a life of genteel poverty.

BRACK: No, well, that's just the problem, isn't it?

TESMAN: Anyway, fortunately it won't be very long now before I'm given my appointment.

BRACK: Well, that sort of thing is quite often a lengthy process.

TESMAN: You haven't heard anything more about it, have you? Mm?

BRACK: No, nothing definite . . . (*Breaks off.*) There is one thing. I do have one piece of news for you.

TESMAN: What?

BRACK: Your old friend, Eilert Lovborg, has arrived in town.

TESMAN: Yes, I know.

BRACK: Oh? How did you find that out?

TESMAN: That friend of Hedda's told us.

BRACK: Oh. What was her name? I didn't catch it.

TESMAN: Mrs Elvsted.

BRACK: Oh, the magistrate's wife. Yes, he's been living up there with them, hasn't he?

TESMAN: Yes, and I was delighted to hear that he'd turned over a new leaf.

BRACK: So they say.

TESMAN: And I gather he's published a new book, hasn't he? Mm?

BRACK: He has, yes.

TESMAN: And it seems to have created something of a sensation.

BRACK: Quite an unusual sensation.

TESMAN: Extraordinary. That's very good news, isn't it? He's exceptionally talented. I was afraid he'd completely gone to pieces.

BRACK: That's what everybody thought.

TESMAN: But what's he going to do now? How's he going to make a living? Mm?

(*As* TESMAN *is finishing his sentence,* HEDDA *enters through the hall door.*)

HEDDA: (*To* BRACK, *laughing with a certain contempt*) Tesman spends his life worrying about how people are going to make a living.

TESMAN: We're just talking about poor Eilert Lovborg, dear.

HEDDA: (*Looking sharply at him*) Oh? (*Sits down in the armchair by the fire and asks casually*) What's the matter with him?

TESMAN: Well, I'm sure he must have frittered away his inheritance ages ago. And he can't very well write a new book every year, can he? Mm? So I was wondering what was going to become of him.

BRACK: I might be able to give you some information about that.

TESMAN: Oh?

BRACK: You must remember his relatives have quite a lot of influence.

29

TESMAN: Yes, but unfortunately his relatives have completely washed their hands of him.

BRACK: At one time he was thought of as the white hope of the family.

TESMAN: Yes, yes, at one time. But he ruined all that himself.

HEDDA: Who knows? (*A thin smile.*) Up there at the Elvsteds', they're supposed to have rescued him.

BRACK: And then there's this book he's published.

TESMAN: Yes, well, I hope to God they can help him find something to do. I've just written to him. I invited him to come and see us this evening, Hedda.

BRACK: But, Tesman, I thought you were coming to my bachelor party this evening. You promised last night, on the quay.

HEDDA: Had you forgotten, Tesman?

TESMAN: Yes. Completely.

BRACK: Anyway, I'm sure he won't come.

TESMAN: What makes you think that? Mm?

BRACK: (*Hesitating, gets up and puts his hands on the back of the chair*) My dear Tesman, and you too, Mrs Tesman, there's something it wouldn't be right to go on concealing from you, it's . . . it's . . .

TESMAN: About Eilert?

BRACK: About you and him.

TESMAN: Well then, you'd better tell us.

BRACK: You ought to be prepared for your appointment not to be quite as automatic as you hope and expect.

TESMAN: (*Jumping up uneasily*) Why, has it been blocked in some way? Mm?

BRACK: It's possible that the award of the post may depend on the results of a competition.

TESMAN: A competition! What about that, Hedda, extraordinary!

HEDDA: (*Leaning further back in her chair*) So that's it . . .

TESMAN: But against whom? Surely not . . .

BRACK: Precisely. Eilert Lovborg.

TESMAN: (*Wringing his hands*) But this is quite inconceivable! It's quite impossible! Isn't it? Mm?

BRACK: All the same, I think that's what's going to happen.

TESMAN: But, I mean, after all, Judge Brack, that would be unbelievably inconsiderate. (*Waves his arms about.*) I mean, I am a married man. And we married because we were counting on that, Hedda and I. Ran up all those debts. And borrowed money from Auntie Julia as well. My God, I'd more or less been promised that job, hadn't I? Mm?

BRACK: Now, calm down, I'm sure you'll get it in the end. After this contest.

HEDDA: (*Motionless in the armchair*) It's rather exciting, isn't it, Tesman? Like a race.

TESMAN: Oh, Hedda, my dear, I don't see how you can be so casual about it.

HEDDA: (*As before*) But I'm not. I'm really quite anxious to see what happens.

BRACK: In any case, Mrs Tesman, I think it's quite a good thing you should know what the position is. Before you start making those little purchases I gather you're threatening.

HEDDA: I don't see what difference this can make.

BRACK: Don't you? Well, that's up to you. Goodbye. (*To* TESMAN) When I take my afternoon walk, I'll call by to collect you.

TESMAN: Yes, do. I don't know what to think about this.

HEDDA: (*Lying down and stretching out a hand*) Goodbye, Judge, come back soon.

BRACK: I will. Goodbye, goodbye.

TESMAN: (*Accompanying him to the door*) Goodbye, Judge, I'm sorry about all this.

(JUDGE BRACK *exits by the hall door.*)

(*Crossing the room*) You see, Hedda, that's what comes of setting off on these romantic adventures, isn't it? Mm?

HEDDA: (*Looks at him, smiling*) Experienced at that, are you?

TESMAN: Well, you must admit it was rather adventurous to marry and set up home on nothing but expectations.

HEDDA: You may be right.

TESMAN: Well, anyway, Hedda, we have our beautiful home. Isn't that true? Our dream house. The house we fell in love with, you might almost say, don't you think, mm?

HEDDA: (*Getting up slowly and wearily*) I thought we agreed we were going to lead an active social life. Open house.

TESMAN: My God, yes, I was really looking forward to that. Seeing you as hostess at the head of your chosen circle. Mm? Yes. Ah, well, for the time being, we shall have to make do with each other, Hedda. And Auntie Julia will be able to come round quite often. But things ought to have been very different for you, very different.

HEDDA: I suppose I shan't be able to have my butler, that'll be the first thing.

TESMAN: I'm afraid not. I'm afraid servants are completely out of the question.

HEDDA: And the horse I was going to have . . .

TESMAN: (*Appalled*) Horse?

HEDDA: . . . I suppose I'd better put that right out of my mind.

TESMAN: Good God, yes, I think that goes without saying.

HEDDA: (*Crossing the room*) Well, anyway, I still have one diversion to keep me going while I'm waiting.

TESMAN: (*Beaming*) Well, I'm very glad to hear it. What's that, Hedda? Mm?

HEDDA: (*In the doorway, watching him with concealed contempt*) My pistols, George.

TESMAN: (*Anxiously*) Your pistols?

HEDDA: (*With cold eyes*) General Gabler's pistols.
(*She exits left through the back room.*)

TESMAN: (*Running over to the door and calling after her*) No, Hedda, my dear, for God's sake, don't play with those dangerous things, don't, Hedda, for my sake, mm?

ACT TWO

*The Tesmans' room, just as it was in Act One, except that the grand
piano has been moved out and replaced by an elegant little writing
table with bookshelves. A small table stands next to the sofa on the
left. Most of the flowers have been taken away. Mrs Elvsted's flowers
are on the large table in the foreground.*

Afternoon. HEDDA, *dressed to receive visitors, is alone in the room.
She is standing by the open glass door, loading one of her pistols. The
other is lying in an open pistol case on the writing table.*

HEDDA: (*Looking down into the garden and calling out*) Hello,
    Judge, back again!

BRACK: (*Calling from a distance*) That's right, Mrs Tesman.

HEDDA: (*Lifting the pistol and aiming*) I think I'll shoot you, Judge
    Brack.

BRACK: (*Calling, still invisible*) Stop it! Don't point that thing at
    me.

HEDDA: This is what comes of trying to creep in the back way.
    (*She fires.*)

BRACK: (*Closer*) Have you gone quite mad . . .?

HEDDA: I didn't hit you. Or did I?

BRACK: (*Still outside*) I wish you wouldn't fool about like that.

HEDDA: Come in, Judge.

    (JUDGE BRACK, *dressed for his bachelor party, comes in through
    the glass door. He carries a light overcoat over his arm.*)

BRACK: My God, I thought you'd given up that game. What are
    you doing?

HEDDA: Oh, I'm just standing here, firing into the blue.

BRACK: (*Gently taking the pistol from her hand*) Allow me. (*Looks
    at it.*) Ah, yes, I know this one well. (*Looks around.*) Where's
    its case? Ah. (*Puts the pistol in the case and closes it.*) Enough
    fun for one day.

HEDDA: Well, for God's sake, what do you suggest I do with
    myself?

BRACK: Haven't there been any visitors?

HEDDA: (*Closing the glass door*) Not one. All our best friends must still be in the country.

BRACK: And Tesman's not at home, is he?

HEDDA: (*At the writing table, putting the pistol case in a drawer and locking it*) No. As soon as he'd eaten, he rushed over to see his aunts. He didn't expect you so early.

BRACK: Ah, why didn't I think of that? How stupid of me.

HEDDA: (*Turning to look at him*) Stupid? Why?

BRACK: Because if I had thought of it, I could have come . . . even earlier.

HEDDA: (*Crossing the room*) There wouldn't have been anyone here if you had. I've been in my room since lunch, changing.

BRACK: Isn't there some sort of a tiny chink in your door, so we could have communicated?

HEDDA: You forgot to arrange for one.

BRACK: That was stupid of me as well.

HEDDA: So we'll just have to settle down here. And wait. Tesman probably won't be home for some time.

BRACK: I expect I shall manage to be patient.

(HEDDA *sits in the corner of the sofa.* BRACK *puts his overcoat over the back of the nearest chair and sits down, keeping his hat in his hands. A short silence. They look at each other.*)

HEDDA: Well?

BRACK: (*In the same tone*) Well?

HEDDA: I asked first.

BRACK: (*Bending forward a little*) Now, let's just have a nice quiet little chat, Hedda.

HEDDA: (*Leaning further back on the sofa*) It seems for ever since we last had a talk, doesn't it? Except for a few words yesterday evening and this morning and I don't count that.

BRACK: Just the two of us, you mean? A private talk.

HEDDA: Yes. Something like that.

BRACK: Every day, when I walked past, I wished you were home again.

HEDDA: And I've spent my whole time wishing the same thing.

BRACK: Have you? Really, Hedda? I thought you were having the

34

most wonderful time abroad.

HEDDA: Is that what you thought?

BRACK: Well, that's what Tesman said in his letters.

HEDDA: Him! His idea of bliss is rooting around in libraries. And sitting copying out old parchments, or whatever you call them.

BRACK: (*Slightly malicious*) Well, I suppose that's what he's been called to do in life. Among other things.

HEDDA: Yes, of course. And I suppose if that's your . . . But what about me? My dear, I've been so desperately bored.

BRACK: (*Sympathetically*) Have you really? Seriously?

HEDDA: Well, just think about it a minute. Six whole months without meeting anyone who knew anything about our friends. Or anyone who could talk about the things that interest us.

BRACK: Yes, I should think I would feel a bit cut off.

HEDDA: But the thing I found absolutely unbearable . . .

BRACK: Yes?

HEDDA: Was always the whole time being with . . . the same one person.

BRACK: (*Nodding in agreement*) Day and night. Yes, I can imagine. All the time.

HEDDA: That's what I said, the whole time.

BRACK: Quite. But he's fairly accommodating, Tesman. I'd have thought you could have . . .

HEDDA: Tesman is . . . an academic.

BRACK: Undeniably.

HEDDA: And academics certainly don't make entertaining travelling companions. Not in the long run, anyway.

BRACK: Not even . . . the academic you love?

HEDDA: Ugh, please don't use that nauseating word.

BRACK: (*Surprised*) What's that, Hedda?

HEDDA: (*Half laughing, half angry*) You just try it. Listening to the history of civilization day and night.

BRACK: The whole time.

HEDDA: Yes. And all that stuff about medieval husbandry. That's really grim, you can't get much worse than that.

BRACK: (*Looking inquiringly at her*) But, then, tell me . . . I mean, I don't really understand why, erm . . .

HEDDA: Why I married George Tesman?

BRACK: Well, if you like, yes.

HEDDA: Do you find it as surprising as that?

BRACK: Yes and no, Hedda.

HEDDA: I'd really danced myself to a standstill, Judge. My time was up. (*A slight shudder.*) No, I mustn't say things like that. Or think them either.

BRACK: You've certainly no reason to.

HEDDA: Ah, reasons. (*Watches him carefully.*) One thing about George Tesman, you must admit he's entirely respectable.

BRACK: Respectable and upright. God, yes.

HEDDA: And I can't think of anything really ridiculous about him, can you?

BRACK: Ridiculous? No, I don't think so, not really.

HEDDA: Well then. And he's extremely conscientious about his research work. I don't see why he shouldn't go quite a long way eventually.

BRACK: (*Looking at her a little uncertainly*) Everyone else expects him to finish up in some exceptionally distinguished position. I thought you did too.

HEDDA: (*With a tired expression*) Yes, I did. And since what he seemed intent on, under any circumstances, was to look after me, I could see no reason to turn him down.

BRACK: No, well, I suppose if you look at it that way . . .

HEDDA: More than any of my other admirers was prepared to do, my dear.

BRACK: (*Laughing*) Well, I certainly can't answer for all the others. But as far as I'm concerned, I've always felt, as you well know, a certain . . . respect for the bonds of matrimony. Generally speaking, anyway, Hedda.

HEDDA: (*Lightly*) Oh, I can assure you, I never pinned any hopes on you.

BRACK: All I want is a warm, friendly environment, where I can make myself useful in all sorts of ways and be free to come and go and know I was regarded as an intimate friend.

HEDDA: By the man of the house, you mean?

BRACK: (*Bowing*) Well, to be quite frank, preferably by the lady. By the man as well, obviously. You see, something like that . . . what I mean is, a triangular relationship like that is really very agreeable for everyone concerned.

HEDDA: Yes, I don't know how often I must have longed for another man to join us while we were away. God, the two of us, stuck in that compartment!

BRACK: Fortunately, your honeymoon is over now. Journey's end.

HEDDA: (*Shaking her head*) There's still a long, long way to go. This is only a station on the line.

BRACK: Well, then, you must jump out. Get some exercise, Hedda.

HEDDA: I never jump out.

BRACK: Don't you? Really?

HEDDA: No. Because there's always someone there . . .

BRACK: (*Laughing*) Trying to see your legs, is that it?

HEDDA: Exactly.

BRACK: Yes, but . . .

HEDDA: (*Rejecting this with a gesture*) I'm not having it. I'd rather stay where I already am. Just the two of us.

BRACK: Suppose another man were to get on and join the happy couple?

HEDDA: Well, now, that would be quite another matter.

BRACK: An intimate, understanding friend . . .

HEDDA: . . . able to be entertaining about all kinds of lively subjects . . .

BRACK: . . . and not remotely academic.

HEDDA: (*Sighing audibly*) Well, that would certainly be a relief.

BRACK: (*Hearing the front door open and glancing towards it*) The triangle is completed.

HEDDA: (*Half aloud*) And the train moves on.

(GEORGE TESMAN, *wearing a grey sports suit and a soft felt hat, enters from the hall. He carries a number of unbound books under his arm and in his pockets.*)

TESMAN: (*Moving towards the table by the corner sofa*) Hoo, warm

work lugging this lot around. (*He puts the books down.*) I'm
dripping with sweat, Hedda. Ah, well, well, Judge, you're
already here, are you? Mm? Berte didn't say.

BRACK: (*Getting up*) I came in through the garden.

HEDDA: What are those books you've got?

TESMAN: (*Standing looking through them*) Just some new books
and periodicals I must catch up on. Academic stuff, you
know.

HEDDA: Academic stuff?

BRACK: Ah, Mrs Tesman, academic stuff.

(BRACK *and* HEDDA *exchange understanding smiles.*)

HEDDA: How many more books and periodicals do you have to
read?

TESMAN: Well, my dear, there's really no limit to it. I have to
keep up with everything that's written and published.

HEDDA: Yes, I suppose so.

TESMAN: (*Looking through the books*) And look, I've managed to
get hold of Eilert Lovborg's new book as well. (*Offers it to
her.*) Perhaps you'd like to have a look at it, Hedda? Mm?

HEDDA: No, thanks. Well, later perhaps.

TESMAN: I had a quick look at it on the way home.

BRACK: And what's your . . . academic opinion?

TESMAN: Seems remarkably sound to me. He's never written like
this before. (*Collects his books.*) I'll just take them into my
study. I always enjoy cutting the pages so much. And then I
must change. (*To* BRACK) We don't need to leave just yet, do
we? Mm?

BRACK: Oh, good Lord, no, no hurry.

TESMAN: Good, then I'll take my time. (*Takes the books with him,
stops in the doorway and turns around.*) By the way, Hedda,
Auntie Julia can't come and see you this evening.

HEDDA: Can't she? Nothing to do with that business about her
hat, is it?

TESMAN: Not at all. I don't know how you can think a thing like
that about Auntie Julia, extraordinary. No, Auntie Rina is
very ill.

HEDDA: She generally is.

TESMAN: Yes, but today she was really quite a lot worse, poor
thing.

HEDDA: Well then, naturally her sister would want to stay and
look after her. And I shall just have to put up with it.

TESMAN: Anyway, you can't imagine how delighted Auntie Julia
was to see you looking so strapping after your travels.

HEDDA: (*Half aloud, getting up*) Oh, these everlasting aunts!

TESMAN: Mm?

HEDDA: (*Moving towards the glass door*) Nothing.

TESMAN: Right.

(*He exits through the back room.*)

BRACK: What was that about a hat?

HEDDA: Miss Tesman's, that was something that happened this
morning. She put her hat down over there on the chair . . .
(*Looks at him and smiles.*) . . . and I pretended I thought it
was the maid's.

BRACK: (*Shaking his head*) But, Hedda, how could you do a thing
like that? To a harmless old lady?

HEDDA: (*Crossing the room nervously*) I don't know. I have these
sudden impulses. And there's nothing I can do about it.
(*Flops down on to the armchair by the stove.*) I can't explain
why.

BRACK: (*Behind the armchair*) You aren't really very happy.
That's why.

HEDDA: (*Looking in front of her*) I can't see any reason why I
should be. Happy. Can you think of a reason?

BRACK: Yes. Several. For one thing, here you are in the house
you wanted so much.

HEDDA: (*Looking up at him and laughing*) You don't believe in that
myth as well, do you?

BRACK: Isn't it true?

HEDDA: Well, there is some truth in it.

BRACK: Go on.

HEDDA: Well, it's true that I used Tesman to escort me home
after dinner parties last summer.

BRACK: Unfortunately, I had to go in a completely different
direction.

HEDDA: Yes, I know you were going in different directions, last summer.

BRACK: (*Laughing*) Really, Hedda, you ought to be ashamed of yourself. Anyway, go on about Tesman.

HEDDA: Well, we came past here one evening. And there was poor Tesman writhing about as usual, groping around trying to think of something to say. So I felt sorry for the man of learning . . .

BRACK: (*A doubting smile*) You did, did you?

HEDDA: Yes, I did. Really. And to help him out of his misery, I just said, quite frivolously, that I'd like to live in this villa.

BRACK: Was that all you said?

HEDDA: Then, yes.

BRACK: And afterwards?

HEDDA: Afterwards, my dear, my frivolity led to other things.

BRACK: Unfortunately, Hedda, frivolity often does.

HEDDA: Thank you. So you see it was this passion for Secretary Falk's villa that forged the first links between George Tesman and me. And that was what led to the engagement and the wedding and the honeymoon and all the rest of it. Yes, Judge . . . I've made my bed and . . . now I must lie in it, I almost said.

BRACK: How wonderful! You mean you really couldn't care less about this place?

HEDDA: God, no.

BRACK: Even though we've made it so comfortable for you?

HEDDA: Ugh, all the rooms stink of lavender and dried roses. Perhaps Auntie Julia brought the smell with her.

BRACK: (*Laughing*) More likely to be a left-over from the late Mrs Falk.

HEDDA: Yes, there is something posthumous about it. Like flowers the morning after the ball. (*Clasps her hands behind her neck, leans back in her chair and looks at him.*) Oh, Judge, you can't imagine how terribly bored I'm going to be here.

BRACK: Why shouldn't we find something to keep you interested, Hedda, some kind of vocation?

HEDDA: Vocation? That would interest me?

BRACK: Well, preferably, yes.

HEDDA: God knows where you'd go to look for that! I often think . . . (*Breaks off.*) But I don't suppose that would work either.

BRACK: It might, tell me.

HEDDA: I was just thinking I might get Tesman to go into politics.

BRACK: (*Laughing*) Tesman? Are you serious? Politics, he'd be hopeless at it, it wouldn't suit him at all.

HEDDA: No, I know, you're probably right. But suppose I pushed him into it anyway?

BRACK: Why? What satisfaction would it give you? He wouldn't be any good at it. So why should you want to push him into it?

HEDDA: Because I'm bored, don't you understand? (*Pause.*) So you think it would be completely impossible for Tesman to become a Minister?

BRACK: Erm, well, Hedda, you must realize, for one thing, even if he wanted to, he'd need to be comparatively rich.

HEDDA: (*Getting up impatiently*) Yes, that's just it, isn't it! It's this miserable penny-pinching I've let myself in for . . . (*Crosses the room.*) That's what makes life so utterly pathetic and absurd. Because it is.

BRACK: I don't think that's where the fault lies.

HEDDA: You don't?

BRACK: The thing is, you've never had a really transforming experience.

HEDDA: You mean something important?

BRACK: You could put it like that. And you may be about to.

HEDDA: (*Tossing her head back*) If you mean the complications about that wretched professorship, that's Tesman's business. I'm not going to waste my time worrying about it.

BRACK: No, no, never mind about that. But suppose you were to find yourself with what might euphemistically be described as an important and . . . heavy responsibility? (*Smiles.*) A new responsibility for little Hedda.

HEDDA: (*Angrily*) Be quiet. You won't see anything like that happen, ever.

BRACK: (*Cautiously*) We'll talk about it again in a year's time, shall we? At the most.

HEDDA: (*Shortly*) My dear Judge, I have no talent for that kind of thing. Or for anything responsible.

BRACK: Don't you think you should have? After all, most women have the talent and the inclination . . .

HEDDA: (*By the glass door*) I said be quiet. I often think there's only one thing in the world I have any talent for.

BRACK: (*Approaching her*) And dare I ask what that is?

HEDDA: (*Standing, looking out*) Boring myself to death. Now you know. (*Turns round, looks over towards the back room and laughs.*) Yes, I was right. Here comes the professor.

BRACK: (*Quietly warning her*) Now, now, Hedda.
    (GEORGE TESMAN, *dressed for the party and carrying his hat and gloves, enters from the right through the back room.*)

TESMAN: Hedda, Eilert Lovborg hasn't sent a message saying he isn't coming, has he? Mm?

HEDDA: No.

TESMAN: Then I expect he'll be here any minute.

BRACK: Do you really think he's going to come?

TESMAN: I'm almost sure he will. What you told us this morning is nothing but idle gossip.

BRACK: Is it?

TESMAN: Well, anyway, Auntie Julia told me she didn't think he'd ever stand in my way again. You see?

BRACK: Oh well, that's all right, then.

TESMAN: (*Putting his hat and gloves on a chair on the right*) Yes, well, I think if you don't mind I'd better wait for him as long as possible.

BRACK: Plenty of time. I'm not expecting anyone before seven or half past.

TESMAN: Good, we can stay and keep Hedda company for a bit. And see what happens. Mm?

HEDDA: (*Moving Brack's overcoat and hat to the corner sofa*) And, if the worst comes to the worst, Mr Lovborg can always stay here with me.

BRACK: (*Trying to take his things*) I'll do that, Mrs Tesman. What do you mean, if the worst comes to the worst?

HEDDA: Well, if he doesn't want to go with you and Tesman.

TESMAN: (*Dubiously*) But, Hedda dear, I don't know if it would be altogether right for him to stay here with you, do you think, mm? Auntie Julia can't come, remember?

HEDDA: Yes, but Mrs Elvsted is coming. The three of us can have a cup of tea together.

TESMAN: Oh, well, that'll be all right.

BRACK: (*Smiling*) Probably safer for him as well.

HEDDA: Why?

BRACK: Good Lord, Mrs Tesman, you've made enough withering remarks in the past about my little bachelor parties. You always used to say they should only be attended by men of the very toughest moral fibre.

HEDDA: I should think Mr Lovborg's moral fibre should be tough enough by now. He is a converted sinner.

(BERTE *appears in the hall doorway.*)

BERTE: Madam, there's a gentleman here to see you.

HEDDA: Yes, show him in.

TESMAN: (*Quietly*) It's him, I'm sure it is. Extraordinary.

(EILERT LOVBORG *enters from the hall. He is slim and lean, the same age as* TESMAN, *but looks older and somewhat the worse for wear. His hair and beard are dark brown, his face is longish and pale, with a few red blotches on his cheekbones. He is wearing an elegant, very new, black suit, and carrying dark gloves and a silk hat. He stops just inside the door and bows abruptly. He seems a little embarrassed.*)

(TESMAN *goes up to him and shakes hands*) Eilert, my dear chap, how nice to see you after all this time.

LOVBORG: (*Subdued*) Thanks for your letter. (*Approaches* HEDDA.) May I shake hands with you as well, Mrs Tesman?

HEDDA: (*Taking his hand*) We're delighted to see you, Mr Lovborg. (*A gesture.*) I don't know if you two . . .

LOVBORG: (*Bowing slightly*) Judge Brack, isn't it?

BRACK: (*The same*) Well. It's been some time . . .

TESMAN: (*To* LOVBORG, *putting his hands on his shoulders*) Now you must make yourself completely at home, Eilert. Mustn't he, Hedda? I gather you're planning to settle in town again, aren't you? Mm?

LOVBORG: I'd like to.

TESMAN: Very wise. Listen, I've managed to get hold of your book. But to tell you the truth I haven't had time to read it yet.

LOVBORG: I should save yourself the trouble.

TESMAN: What do you mean? Why?

LOVBORG: Because it isn't much good.

TESMAN: Extraordinary thing to say.

BRACK: But I thought it had been very well received.

LOVBORG: I intended it to be. So when I wrote the book, I made sure everyone would be able to follow it.

BRACK: Sounds reasonable.

TESMAN: Yes, but, Eilert . . .

LOVBORG: Because now I want to try to re-establish myself. Make a fresh start.

TESMAN: (*Slightly embarrassed*) Ah, that's it, is it? Mm?

LOVBORG: (*Smiling, putting down his hat and taking a parcel wrapped in paper from his coat pocket*) But when this comes out, George Tesman, this one you must read. Because this is a real book. The first one I've put myself into.

TESMAN: Is it? What's it about?

LOVBORG: It's the sequel.

TESMAN: Sequel? What of?

LOVBORG: My book.

TESMAN: Your new book?

LOVBORG: That's right.

TESMAN: Yes, but, Eilert, I thought that covered everything up to the present day.

LOVBORG: It does. This one's about the future.

TESMAN: The future? But, I mean, we don't know anything about that.

LOVBORG: No. Even so, there are one or two things to be said about it. (*Opens the parcel.*) Here, have a look.

TESMAN: That's not your writing.

LOVBORG: I dictated it. (*Looks through the pages.*) It's in two sections. The first deals with what will be the formative influences on future civilizations. And this second part here ... (*Goes on sorting through the pages.*) ... is about the shape those civilizations will take.

TESMAN: Amazing. It would never occur to me to write about anything like that.

HEDDA: (*By the glass door, drumming on the pane*) No.

LOVBORG: (*Wrapping the manuscript up again and putting the parcel on the table*) I brought it with me because I thought I'd read some of it to you this evening.

TESMAN: Well, it was very kind of you. The only thing is ... (*Looks at* BRACK.) I don't see how we can fit it in this evening.

LOVBORG: Never mind, some other time. There's no hurry.

BRACK: I should explain, Mr Lovborg, we're having a little party at my house this evening. You know, in honour of Tesman really ...

LOVBORG: (*Looking round for his hat*) Oh, well, in that case, I won't ...

BRACK: No, listen, I'd be very pleased if you could join us.

LOVBORG: (*Shortly and decisively*) No, I can't. Thank you very much.

BRACK: Oh, come on. Please do. We shan't be more than a chosen few. I'm sure it'll all be very lively, as Hed– ... um, Mrs Tesman always says.

LOVBORG: I'm sure it will. All the same, I ...

BRACK: And you could bring your manuscript and read it to Tesman at my place. I have plenty of rooms.

TESMAN: Yes, what about that, Eilert, you could do that, couldn't you? Mm?

HEDDA: (*Intervening*) But suppose Mr Lovborg doesn't want to, dear? I'm sure Mr Lovborg would rather stay here and have dinner with me.

LOVBORG: (*Looking at her*) With you, Mrs Tesman?

HEDDA: And Mrs Elvsted.

LOVBORG: Oh. (*Casually.*) Yes, I saw her for a minute this morning.

45

HEDDA: Did you? Yes, she's coming over. So that means you're more or less obliged to stay, Mr Lovborg. Otherwise, she'll have no one to see her home.

LOVBORG: I see. All right, thank you very much, Mrs Tesman, I will stay.

HEDDA: I'll just go and tell the maid.

(*She goes over to the hall door and rings.* BERTE *enters.* HEDDA *speaks quietly to her, pointing towards the back room.* BERTE *nods and exits.*)

TESMAN: (*While this is going on*) Erm, Eilert, is it this new subject, I mean all this about the future, that you're going to lecture on?

LOVBORG: Yes.

TESMAN: They told me in the bookshop you were going to give a course of lectures this autumn.

LOVBORG: Yes, I am. You can't really blame me for accepting.

TESMAN: No, of course not, my God. It's just that . . .

LOVBORG: I can see you must find it rather upsetting.

TESMAN: (*Dejectedly*) I could hardly expect you to . . . erm, just for my sake . . .

LOVBORG: But I shall wait until you've been given your appointment.

TESMAN: Wait? Yes, but . . . yes, but . . . isn't there going to be this competition? Mm?

LOVBORG: No . . . All I want is to outclass you. In public opinion.

TESMAN: Good heavens, Auntie Julia was right all along. I knew it, I knew it. What about that, Hedda, can you imagine, Eilert Lovborg isn't going to stand in our way.

HEDDA: Our way? It's nothing to do with me.

(*She moves towards the back room, where* BERTE *is putting a tray of decanters and glasses on the table.* HEDDA *nods approval and returns.* BERTE *exits.*)

TESMAN: (*While this is going on*) What about you, Judge Brack, what do you think about all this? Mm?

BRACK: Well, I think to outclass someone is all very commendable, er . . .

TESMAN: Oh, yes, it is. Certainly. Even so . . .

HEDDA: (*Looking at* TESMAN *and smiling coldly*) You look as if you'd been struck by lightning.

TESMAN: Yes. I feel a bit . . . like that.

BRACK: Well, after all, a thunderstorm has just passed over us, Mrs Tesman.

HEDDA: (*Pointing towards the back room*) Wouldn't you all like to go in and have a glass of cold punch?

BRACK: (*Looking at his watch*) Before we go? Wouldn't do any harm.

TESMAN: Marvellous idea, Hedda, marvellous! Now I'm in such a good mood . . .

HEDDA: And you, Mr Lovborg, please.

LOVBORG: (*Gesture of refusal*) No, thank you. Not for me.

BRACK: Good Lord, there's nothing poisonous about a drop of cold punch.

LOVBORG: Perhaps not for some people.

HEDDA: Never mind, I'll take care of Mr Lovborg.

TESMAN: Yes, do, Hedda dear, would you?

(*He and* BRACK *go into the back room, sit down, drink punch, light cigarettes and talk animatedly during the following scene.* LOVBORG *remains standing by the stove.* HEDDA *goes over to the writing table.*)

HEDDA: (*In a rather loud voice*) I'll show you some photographs, shall I, would you like that? Tesman and I passed through the Tyrol on our way home.

(*She fetches an album, puts it on the table by the sofa, and then sits in the far corner of the sofa.* LOVBORG *approaches, stops and looks at her. Then he fetches a chair and sits down on her left with his back to the back room. She opens the album.*)

Now. You see this mountain range here, Mr Lovborg? It's the Ortler range. Tesman's written the names underneath. Here we are. The Ortler range. Near Meran.

LOVBORG: (*Who has been watching her carefully, now speaks quietly and slowly*) Hedda . . . Gabler.

HEDDA: (*Looking up sharply*) What? Ssh!

LOVBORG: (*Repeats softly*) Hedda Gabler.

47

HEDDA: (*Looking at the album*) Yes, that was my name once.
   When . . . you and I used to know each other.

LOVBORG: So from now on for the rest of my life I must learn to
   stop saying Hedda Gabler.

HEDDA: (*Continuing to turn the pages*) Yes, you must. And I think
   you ought to start practising. The sooner the better, I'd say.

LOVBORG: (*Indignantly*) Hedda Gabler married. And to George
   Tesman!

HEDDA: Yes. That's the way things happen.

LOVBORG: Oh, Hedda, Hedda, how could you throw yourself
   away like that?

HEDDA: (*Looking at him sharply*) What? That's enough of that.

LOVBORG: What do you mean?

   (TESMAN *enters and approaches the sofa.*)

HEDDA: (*Hearing him coming, adopts a neutral tone*) And this, Mr
   Lovborg, is taken from the d'Ampezzo Valley. Look at those
   rock formations. (*Looks up at* TESMAN *affectionately.*) What's
   the name of that peculiar range, dear?

TESMAN: Let's have a look. Oh yes, those are the Dolomites.

HEDDA: That's right. Those are the Dolomites, Mr Lovborg.

TESMAN: Hedda, I was just wondering if you wouldn't like us to
   bring in some punch anyway. I mean, for you. Mm?

HEDDA: Yes, why don't you, thanks. And perhaps a few biscuits.

TESMAN: Cigarettes?

HEDDA: No.

TESMAN: Right.

   (*He goes into the back room and moves across to the right.*
   BRACK *is sitting there and glancing from time to time at* HEDDA
   and LOVBORG.)

LOVBORG: (*Quietly as before*) Now, tell me, Hedda. How could
   you do a thing like this?

HEDDA: (*Pretending to be absorbed in the album*) If you go on
   calling me Hedda, I shan't want to talk to you at all.

LOVBORG: Can't I even call you Hedda when we're alone?

HEDDA: No. You can think it. But you mustn't say it.

LOVBORG: I see. It's an insult to your love . . . for George
   Tesman, is it?

HEDDA: (*Looks at him, smiling*) Love? Don't be ridiculous.

LOVBORG: You don't love him, then?

HEDDA: That doesn't mean I'd ever be unfaithful to him. Because I wouldn't.

LOVBORG: Just tell me one thing . . .

HEDDA: Ssh!

(TESMAN *enters from the back room with a small tray.*)

TESMAN: Here you are. Goodies.

(*He puts the tray down on the table.*)

HEDDA: Why are you serving it yourself?

TESMAN: (*Filling the glasses*) I think it's such fun doing things for you, Hedda.

HEDDA: Now you've filled both glasses. Mr Lovborg doesn't want any.

TESMAN: No, but Mrs Elvsted will probably be here soon.

HEDDA: Oh, yes, Mrs Elvsted . . .

TESMAN: You hadn't forgotten her, had you? Mm?

HEDDA: We've been so engrossed in this. (*Shows him a photo.*) Do you remember this little village?

TESMAN: Oh, yes, it's the one at the bottom of the Brenner Pass. Where we spent the night . . .

HEDDA: . . . and met all those lively summer visitors.

TESMAN: Yes, that's right. I only wish we'd had you with us, Eilert. Yes.

(*He goes into the back room and sits down with* BRACK *again.*)

LOVBORG: Will you just tell me one thing . . .

HEDDA: What?

LOVBORG: Was there no love in your feeling for me either? Was there no trace, no spark of love at all?

HEDDA: I don't know. I wonder. I saw us as two soul mates. Two really close friends. (*Smiles.*) I remember you were always very candid.

LOVBORG: That was what you wanted.

HEDDA: When I look back on it, I often feel there was something beautiful, something appealing . . . something courageous . . . about our secret closeness and about having a friendship that no one in the world suspected.

LOVBORG: Yes, there was, wasn't there? I used to come and spend the afternoon at your father's. And the General used to sit by the window, reading the paper. With his back to us.

HEDDA: And we used to sit on the sofa in the corner . . .

LOVBORG: Always with the same magazine open in front of us.

HEDDA: Not having a photograph album.

LOVBORG: Yes. And I used to make my confession to you. And tell you things about myself that no one else knew anything about. Used to sit there admitting I'd been out celebrating all day and night. Always to excess. What kind of power did you have over me to make me want to confide in you like that?

HEDDA: Did I have any power over you?

LOVBORG: Yes, I can't explain it any other way. And all those . . . enigmatic questions you used to ask me . . .

HEDDA: Which you always understood immediately . . .

LOVBORG: How could you sit there and ask me questions like that? Quite openly?

HEDDA: Enigmatically, you just said.

LOVBORG: Yes, but openly as well. Asking me about all those things.

HEDDA: How could you answer, Mr Lovborg?

LOVBORG: Well, exactly, when I think about it now, I can't understand it either. Tell me, wasn't love the basis of our friendship? Didn't you want to absolve me when I came to confess to you? Wasn't that it?

HEDDA: Not quite, no.

LOVBORG: What were your motives, then?

HEDDA: Do you really find it so difficult to understand? A young girl, given the chance, with no danger of being found out . . .

LOVBORG: Yes?

HEDDA: . . . wanting to catch a glimpse of a world . . .

LOVBORG: Go on.

HEDDA: . . . a world she's not allowed to know anything about.

LOVBORG: So that was it?

HEDDA: That was part of it. Something like that.

LOVBORG: We shared an appetite for life. Why shouldn't that, at least, have lasted?

HEDDA: That was your fault.

LOVBORG: You finished it.

HEDDA: Yes, because there was a growing danger that our relationship would be invaded by reality. You should be ashamed, Eilert Lovborg. How could you try to take advantage of your . . . trusting friend?

LOVBORG: (*Clenching his fists*) Why didn't you do it? You threatened to shoot me, why didn't you?

HEDDA: Because I'm terrified of scandal.

LOVBORG: Yes, Hedda. You're a coward, really, aren't you?

HEDDA: A dreadful coward. (*Change of tone*) Luckily for you. Anyway, I see you've found true consolation at the Elvsteds'.

LOVBORG: I know Thea has confided in you.

HEDDA: And I expect you've confided in her. About us.

LOVBORG: I haven't said a word. She's too stupid to understand a thing like that.

HEDDA: Stupid?

LOVBORG: Stupid about that kind of thing.

HEDDA: And I'm a coward. (*Leans towards him, avoiding his eyes and speaks more quietly.*) But now I'm going to confide something to you.

LOVBORG: (*Eagerly*) What?

HEDDA: My not daring to shoot you . . .

LOVBORG: Yes?

HEDDA: . . . wasn't my most cowardly failure . . . that evening.

LOVBORG: (*Looking at her for a moment before understanding and whispering passionately*) Oh, Hedda! Hedda Gabler! So there was something hidden behind our friendship, I can see that now. You and I . . . You were greedy for life as well.

HEDDA: (*Quietly, with a sharp glance*) Be careful. Don't jump to any conclusions.

(*It is getting dark.* BERTE *opens the hall door from the outside.*)
(HEDDA *Snaps the album shut, smiles and calls out*) At last! Thea, my dear, come in.

(MRS ELVSTED *enters from the hall. She is wearing an evening dress. The door is closed behind her.*)

(*From the sofa, stretching her arms out towards her*) Thea, I've been longing to see you!

(MRS ELVSTED *exchanges brief greetings with the men in the back room as she passes, crosses to the table and shakes hands with* HEDDA. LOVBORG *has stood up. He and* MRS ELVSTED *acknowledge each other with a silent nod.*)

MRS ELVSTED: Perhaps I should go and have a word with your husband?

HEDDA: I shouldn't. I should leave them alone. They'll be going soon.

MRS ELVSTED: Going?

HEDDA: Yes, they're going out on a drinking bout.

MRS ELVSTED: (*Quickly, to* LOVBORG) You're not going, are you?

LOVBORG: No.

HEDDA: Mr Lovborg's staying here with us.

MRS ELVSTED: (*Taking a chair and preparing to sit next to him*) It's so good to be here.

HEDDA: No, Thea, not there, please. Come over here next to me. I want to sit between you.

MRS ELVSTED: Just as you like.

(*She walks round the table and sits on the sofa on* HEDDA'*s right.* LOVBORG *sits down in his chair again.*)

LOVBORG: (*After a short pause, to* HEDDA) Isn't she beautiful to look at?

HEDDA: (*Gently stroking her hair*) Only to look at?

LOVBORG: Yes. The two of us, she and I, are soul mates. We trust each other implicitly. It means we can sit and discuss things really openly . . .

HEDDA: No enigmas, Mr Lovborg?

LOVBORG: Well . . .

MRS ELVSTED: (*Softly, clinging on to* HEDDA) I'm so happy, Hedda. He says I've inspired him.

HEDDA: (*Looking at her with a smile*) No, does he say that?

LOVBORG: The way she does things, Mrs Tesman, she has such courage.

MRS ELVSTED: Courage, me!

LOVBORG: Unlimited courage, when it comes to helping your friend.

HEDDA: Ah, courage. If only I had some.

LOVBORG: What do you mean?

HEDDA: Then perhaps life would be worth living. (*Changes the subject abruptly.*) Now, Thea dear, you must have a nice glass of cold punch.

MRS ELVSTED: No, thank you, I don't.

HEDDA: Well, what about you, Mr Lovborg?

LOVBORG: No, thanks, I don't either.

MRS ELVSTED: He doesn't either.

HEDDA: (*Looking at him hard*) What if I wanted you to?

LOVBORG: Wouldn't make any difference.

HEDDA: (*Laughing*) Poor me, have I no power over you at all?

LOVBORG: Not as far as this is concerned.

HEDDA: I still think you should. Seriously. For your sake.

MRS ELVSTED: Hedda . . .

LOVBORG: Why?

HEDDA: Or rather for other people's sake.

LOVBORG: What do you mean?

HEDDA: Otherwise people might get the impression that secretly you're not really being honest and that you haven't any confidence in yourself.

MRS ELVSTED: (*Quietly*) Hedda, don't . . .

LOVBORG: They can think what they like.

MRS ELVSTED: (*Enthusiastically*) Yes!

HEDDA: It's just that looking at Judge Brack a moment ago, I could see it so clearly.

LOVBORG: See what?

HEDDA: The contempt in his smile when you didn't dare join them in there.

LOVBORG: Didn't dare? Obviously I preferred to stay here and talk to you.

MRS ELVSTED: There's nothing surprising about that, is there, Hedda?

HEDDA: No, but that wouldn't be likely to occur to Judge Brack. And I also noticed he couldn't help smiling and catching Tesman's eye when you didn't dare agree to go to his miserable little party.

LOVBORG: Didn't dare? Do you think I didn't dare?

HEDDA: I don't. But that's what Judge Brack thought.

LOVBORG: Well, let him.

HEDDA: So you're not going then?

LOVBORG: I'm staying here with you and Thea.

MRS ELVSTED: Of course he is, Hedda.

HEDDA: (*Smiling and nodding at* LOVBORG) Solid foundations. Principles firm to the last. That's how a man should be. (*Turns to* MRS ELVSTED, *caressing her.*) You see, isn't that what I told you this morning, when you came in so upset . . .?

LOVBORG: (*Taken aback*) Upset?

MRS ELVSTED: (*Terrified*) Hedda . . .

HEDDA: You can see now, can't you? There was no need for all that desperate worry . . . (*Breaks off.*) And now, let's enjoy ourselves, shall we?

LOVBORG: (*Shuddering*) Oh, what is all this, Mrs Tesman?

MRS ELVSTED: Oh, God, Hedda! What are you saying? What are you doing?

HEDDA: Calm down. That abominable Judge is sitting staring at you.

LOVBORG: Desperate worry. About me.

MRS ELVSTED: (*Quietly, miserably*) Oh, Hedda, you've made me terribly unhappy.

LOVBORG: (*Looking at her intently for a moment, face contorted*) That's what we call a friend's implicit trust.

MRS ELVSTED: (*Imploringly*) Just listen to me for a minute . . .

LOVBORG: (*Taking one of the full glasses of punch, raising it and speaking quietly and hoarsely*) Here's to you, Thea! (*He empties the glass, puts it down and takes the other.*)

MRS ELVSTED: (*Quietly*) Oh, Hedda, why should you want this to happen?

HEDDA: Me? Want it? Are you mad?

LOVBORG: And here's to you, Mrs Tesman. Thank you for telling me the truth. Here's to the truth! (*He drinks and goes to fill the glass again.*)

HEDDA: (*Putting her hand on his arm*) No more just now. Remember you're going out to dinner.

MRS ELVSTED: No, no, he isn't!

HEDDA: Ssh! They're looking at you.

LOVBORG: (*Putting the glass down*) Listen, Thea . . . now I do want the truth . . .

MRS ELVSTED: Yes.

LOVBORG: Did your husband know you were coming after me?

MRS ELVSTED: (*Wringing her hands*) Oh, Hedda, did you hear what he said?

LOVBORG: Was it something you worked out between you, your coming into town to watch over me? Or perhaps it was his idea, perhaps he persuaded you to come? He probably needed me in his office, is that it? Or did he miss me at the card table?

MRS ELVSTED: (*Quietly, suffering*) Oh, Lovborg . . .

LOVBORG: (*Picking up the glass and moving to fill it*) Here's to the old magistrate while we're at it.

HEDDA: (*Preventing him*) No more now. Remember you're going out and you're going to read your book to Tesman.

LOVBORG: (*Calm, putting the glass down*) That was stupid of me, Thea, just now. Reacting like that, I mean. Don't be angry with me, my dear friend. You'll see, you and the others, even if I was far gone once, now, I've pulled myself back. With your help, Thea.

MRS ELVSTED: (*Glowing*) Thank God . . .!

(*In the meantime,* BRACK *has consulted his watch. He and* TESMAN *rise and move into the drawing room.*)

BRACK: (*Taking his hat and overcoat*) Well, Mrs Tesman, time we were on our way.

HEDDA: I suppose it is.

LOVBORG: (*Getting up*) I'll come with you, Judge Brack . . .

MRS ELVSTED: (*Quietly and imploringly*) Don't, Lovborg, please . . .

HEDDA: (*Pinching her arm*) They can hear you!

MRS ELVSTED: (*A faint cry*) Ow!

LOVBORG: (*To* BRACK) . . . as you were kind enough to invite me.

BRACK: Changed your mind, then?

LOVBORG: Yes, if that's all right with you.

BRACK: Good, I'm delighted.

LOVBORG: (*Picking up his parcel; to* TESMAN) There are one or two things I'd like to show you before I hand it in.

TESMAN: Well, that'll be very interesting. The only thing is, Hedda, how are we going to get Mrs Elvsted home? Mm?

HEDDA: Oh, I'm sure we'll manage.

LOVBORG: (*Looking over at the women*) Mrs Elvsted? Obviously I must come back and collect her. (*Approaches her.*) About ten o'clock, Mrs Tesman? Will that be all right?

HEDDA: Yes, of course. Perfectly all right.

TESMAN: Well, then, that's arranged. But you mustn't expect me that early, Hedda.

HEDDA: My dear, you can stay as long . . . as long as you like.

MRS ELVSTED: (*Trying to conceal her anxiety*) So I'll . . . wait for you here, shall I, Mr Lovborg?

LOVBORG: (*Hat in hand*) That's right, Mrs Elvsted.

BRACK: So, gentlemen, the mystery train is pulling out. I'm hoping it'll all be very lively, as a certain charming lady always says.

HEDDA: I wish that charming lady could be there, invisible.

BRACK: Why invisible?

HEDDA: To hear some of your lively conversations unabridged, Judge.

BRACK: (*Laughing*) I really wouldn't recommend that to any charming lady.

TESMAN: (*Also laughing*) My word, Hedda, that's a good one! Extraordinary.

BRACK: Well, goodbye, ladies.

LOVBORG: (*Bowing as he leaves*) See you about ten.

(BRACK, LOVBORG *and* TESMAN *leave by the hall door. At the same time* BERTE *enters from the back room with a lighted lamp, which she puts on the living-room table before exiting the same way.*)

MRS ELVSTED: (*Having got up, pacing restlessly around the room*) Hedda, what's going to happen now?

HEDDA: Ten o'clock. He'll be here. I can see him now. Vine leaves in his hair. Burning with courage.

56

MRS ELVSTED: I hope so.

HEDDA: And, don't you see, then he'll be in control of himself again. And he'll be a free man for the rest of his life.

MRS ELVSTED: Oh, God, I only hope you're right.

HEDDA: It'll all be exactly as I say. (*Gets up and moves nearer to* MRS ELVSTED.) You can doubt him as much as you like. I believe in him. And now we shall see which of us is right.

MRS ELVSTED: You must have some ulterior motive in all this, Hedda.

HEDDA: Yes, I have. For once in my life I want the power to control a human destiny.

MRS ELVSTED: Haven't you got that?

HEDDA: No, I haven't. I never have had.

MRS ELVSTED: What about your husband?

HEDDA: Do you really think he's worth the effort? I wish you could understand how poor I am. And you've finished up so rich. (*Puts her arms round her passionately*.) I think I shall set fire to your hair after all.

MRS ELVSTED: Let go! Let me go! I'm frightened of you, Hedda.

BERTE: (*In the doorway*) Tea's ready in the dining room, madam.

HEDDA: Good. We're coming.

MRS ELVSTED: No, no, I'm not. I'd rather go home alone. Now.

HEDDA: Nonsense! You're going to have tea first, you little numbskull. And then, at ten o'clock, Eilert Lovborg will arrive . . . with vine leaves in his hair.

(*She virtually forces* MRS ELVSTED *towards the doorway*.)

ACT THREE

The Tesmans' room. The curtains in the doorway to the back room and in front of the glass door are drawn. The lamp is on the table, turned down and shaded to give a dim light. The stove door is open and we can see the remains of a fire, which has almost burnt itself out.

MRS ELVSTED, *wrapped in a large shawl and resting her feet on a stool, is sitting near the stove, leaning back in an armchair.* HEDDA *is lying fully dressed on the sofa, covered by a blanket. After a pause,* MRS ELVSTED *suddenly sits up in her chair and listens anxiously. Then she sinks back again wearily, moaning softly.*

MRS ELVSTED: Still not back! Oh, God, God . . . still.
    (BERTE *tiptoes cautiously in from the hall door, carrying a letter.*)
    (*Turning and whispering tensely*) Is anyone back yet?
BERTE: (*Quietly*) Yes, a girl just arrived with this letter.
MRS ELVSTED: (*Quickly, stretching out her hand*) A letter? Give it to me!
BERTE: No, it's for the doctor, madam.
MRS ELVSTED: Oh.
BERTE: Miss Tesman's maid brought it. I'll put it here on the table.
MRS ELVSTED: Yes, do.
BERTE: (*Putting the letter on the table*) I think I'd better put the lamp out. It's starting to smoke.
MRS ELVSTED: Yes, I should. It'll soon be light.
BERTE: It is light, madam.
MRS ELVSTED: Dawn already. And no one's back yet.
BERTE: Good Lord, no, I thought that's what it would be.
MRS ELVSTED: Did you?
BERTE: Well, when I heard a certain gentleman had come back to town and when he went off with them . . . We used to hear enough about him in the old days.
MRS ELVSTED: Don't speak so loud. You'll wake up Mrs Tesman.

BERTE: (*Looking at the sofa and sighing*) Oh, dear, poor thing, we'll let her sleep a bit longer. Shall I put a bit more on the fire?

MRS ELVSTED: No, thanks, I'm warm enough.

BERTE: All right.

(*She exits quietly by the hall door.*)

HEDDA: (*Waking up when the door shuts and looking around*) Who's that . . . ?

MRS ELVSTED: Only the maid.

HEDDA: (*Looking around*) What are . . . ? Oh, yes, I remember. (*Sits up on the sofa, stretching and rubbing her eyes.*) What time is it, Thea?

MRS ELVSTED: (*Looking at her watch*) After seven.

HEDDA: What time did Tesman get in?

MRS ELVSTED: He hasn't come back yet.

HEDDA: Still not back?

MRS ELVSTED: (*Getting up*) No one is.

HEDDA: But we stayed up waiting till four o'clock.

MRS ELVSTED: (*Wringing her hands*) I've been waiting for him all night.

HEDDA: (*Yawning and speaking with her hand in front of her mouth*) We might have saved ourselves the trouble.

MRS ELVSTED: Did you manage to get some sleep?

HEDDA: Yes. I think I slept quite well. Didn't you?

MRS ELVSTED: Not a wink. I couldn't, Hedda! I couldn't possibly.

HEDDA: (*Getting up and moving towards her*) Don't worry, there's nothing to worry about. I know exactly what's happened.

MRS ELVSTED: What? Tell me.

HEDDA: Well, presumably, it's just dragged on endlessly at the Judge's . . .

MRS ELVSTED: Well, yes, obviously. Even so . . .

HEDDA: And I expect Tesman didn't dare come home and wake everyone up ringing the bell in the middle of the night. (*Laughs.*) He probably didn't want to show his face either . . . after all that celebrating.

MRS ELVSTED: But . . . where else could he have gone?

HEDDA: I expect he's gone over to his aunts' and slept there.
They keep his old room ready for him.

MRS ELVSTED: No, he can't have stayed there. A letter just
arrived for him from Miss Tesman. There.

HEDDA: Really? (*Looks at the handwriting on the envelope.*) Yes,
that's Aunt Julia's writing. Well, he must have stayed at the
Judge's then. And Eilert Lovborg is sitting there, with vine
leaves in his hair, reading aloud.

MRS ELVSTED: Oh, Hedda, you're just saying that, you don't
believe it.

HEDDA: You really are a little idiot, Thea.

MRS ELVSTED: I'm sorry, I suppose I am.

HEDDA: You look desperately tired.

MRS ELVSTED: Yes, I am desperately tired.

HEDDA: Well then, do as you're told. Go up to my room and lie
down for a bit.

MRS ELVSTED: No, no, I couldn't sleep now.

HEDDA: Of course you can.

MRS ELVSTED: All right, but your husband's bound to get back
soon. And when he does, I want to know straight away . . .

HEDDA: I'll tell you as soon as he gets in.

MRS ELVSTED: Promise, Hedda?

HEDDA: Yes, I promise. Now go up and get some sleep.

MRS ELVSTED: Thank you. I'll try.

(*She exits through the back room.* HEDDA *goes over to the glass
door and draws back the curtains. Daylight streams into the
room. She picks up a small mirror from the writing table, looks at
herself in it and tidies her hair. She goes over to the hall door and
presses the bell. After a short pause,* BERTE *appears.*)

BERTE: Yes, madam?

HEDDA: Put some more wood on the stove, will you? I'm
freezing.

BERTE: Won't take a minute to get warm. (*Rakes the fire and puts
a block of wood on it. Standing listening.*) That was the front
door, wasn't it, madam?

HEDDA: Go and answer it then. I'll look after the fire.

BERTE: It'll catch in no time.

(*She exits through the hall door.* HEDDA *kneels on the footstool and puts some more blocks of wood on the fire. A moment later,* TESMAN *enters from the hall. He looks tired and rather solemn. He tiptoes towards the doorway and is about to slip through the curtains.*)

HEDDA: (*Without looking up from the stove*) Morning.

TESMAN: (*Turning*) Hedda! (*Approaches her.*) Good gracious me, up so early? Mm?

HEDDA: Yes, I got up very early this morning.

TESMAN: Extraordinary. I was sure you'd still be in bed.

HEDDA: Don't talk so loud, Mrs Elvsted is lying down in my room.

TESMAN: Did Mrs Elvsted stay the night here?

HEDDA: Well, no one came to fetch her.

TESMAN: No, I suppose not.

HEDDA: (*Shutting the stove door and getting up*) Well, did you enjoy yourself at the Judge's?

TESMAN: Were you worried about me? Mm?

HEDDA: Certainly not. I just wondered if you enjoyed yourself.

TESMAN: Yes, I did. For once. Especially at the beginning of the evening. When Eilert read to me. We arrived more than an hour early, if you can imagine. And Brack had a lot to see to. So Eilert read to me.

HEDDA: (*Sitting down on the right of the table*) Tell me about it . . .

TESMAN: (*Sitting on the footstool by the stove*) Oh, Hedda, you couldn't begin to imagine what that book will be like. It must be one of the most remarkable books ever written. Extraordinary.

HEDDA: No, no, I didn't really mean that . . .

TESMAN: I have a confession to make, Hedda. When he'd finished reading, something really ugly happened to me.

HEDDA: Ugly?

TESMAN: I sat there envying Eilert for being able to write like that. Can you imagine, Hedda?

HEDDA: I can, yes.

TESMAN: And the terrible thing is that he has all that talent, and yet he's absolutely irredeemable.

HEDDA: Do you mean because he has more courage than the others?

TESMAN: No, I mean because he's quite incapable of doing anything in moderation.

HEDDA: So what happened in the end?

TESMAN: Well, I think it became rather what might be described as bacchanalian.

HEDDA: And did he have vine leaves in his hair?

TESMAN: Vine leaves? I didn't notice any. But he made a long, incoherent speech about the woman who had inspired him in his work. Yes, that's how he put it.

HEDDA: Did he mention her name?

TESMAN: No, he didn't. But I can't think it could be anyone else but Mrs Elvsted. Take my word for it.

HEDDA: Where did you leave him?

TESMAN: On the way into town. It broke up, and the last of us all left at the same time. Brack came with us to get a bit of fresh air. And in the end, you see, we agreed to take Eilert home. He had rather overdone it.

HEDDA: I suppose he had.

TESMAN: Now, this is the really funny thing, Hedda. Or perhaps tragic is a better word for it. I feel almost too ashamed, on Eilert's behalf, to tell you about it . . .

HEDDA: Oh, get on with it . . .

TESMAN: Well, you see, as we were coming into town, I just happened to drop back a bit behind the others. Only for a couple of minutes, if you can imagine . . .

HEDDA: Yes, yes, for goodness' sake . . .

TESMAN: And then, when I was hurrying to catch up with the others, do you know what I found lying on the pavement? Mm?

HEDDA: How could I know?

TESMAN: You mustn't tell anyone about this, Hedda. Do you understand? Promise you won't, for Eilert's sake. (*Takes a parcel wrapped in paper from his coat pocket.*) This is what I found. Now, what do you think?

HEDDA: Isn't that the parcel he had with him yesterday?

TESMAN: Yes, it's the whole of his priceless, irreplaceable manuscript. He'd lost it without realizing. It's extraordinary, Hedda. It's tragic . . .

HEDDA: Why didn't you give it back to him straight away?

TESMAN: I didn't dare. The state he was in . . .

HEDDA: You didn't tell any of the others you'd found it?

TESMAN: Of course not. I didn't want to, you see, for Eilert's sake.

HEDDA: So nobody knows that you have Eilert Lovborg's manuscript.

TESMAN: No. And nobody must find out about it either.

HEDDA: What did you say to him afterwards?

TESMAN: I didn't get a chance to say anything to him. When we got into town, he and two or three others suddenly vanished, just like that. It was extraordinary.

HEDDA: Really? They must have taken him home.

TESMAN: Yes, I suppose they must have. Brack disappeared as well.

HEDDA: And where have you been lurking about since then?

TESMAN: Well, one of our merry company invited some of us back to his place for morning coffee. Or perhaps I should say night coffee, mm? Anyway, as soon as I've had a little rest, and given Eilert a chance to sleep it off a bit, poor chap, I must go round and give this back to him.

HEDDA: (*Reaching out for the parcel*) No, don't give it back yet. I mean, not just yet. Let me read it first.

TESMAN: No, Hedda, my dear, really, I daren't do that, honestly.

HEDDA: You daren't?

TESMAN: No, surely you realize how desperate he'll be when he wakes up and finds the manuscript missing. There's no copy of it, you know. He told me there wasn't.

HEDDA: (*Looking hard at him*) But that sort of book could be rewritten, couldn't it? And come out much the same.

TESMAN: No, I don't think that would ever work. It's the inspiration, you see . . .

HEDDA: Yes, I suppose you're right . . . (*Casually*) Incidentally, there's a letter for you.

63

TESMAN: There isn't, is there?

HEDDA: (*Handing it to him*) It arrived this morning, early.

TESMAN: Oh, it's from Auntie Julia. I wonder what it is. (*Puts the parcel on the other footstool, opens the letter, reads it and leaps up.*) Oh, Hedda, she says poor Auntie Rina is dying.

HEDDA: We've been expecting that, haven't we?

TESMAN: And that if I want to see her again, I shall have to hurry. I'd better race up there this minute.

HEDDA: (*Suppressing a smile*) On your marks.

TESMAN: I wish you could bring yourself to come with me, Hedda dear. Won't you consider it?

TESMAN: (*Getting up and speaking wearily but decisively*) No, don't ask me to. I don't want to look at sickness and death. Or anything ugly, I don't want anything to do with it.

TESMAN: Well . . . (*Bustles around.*) Where's my hat? And my coat, where are they? Ah yes. I only hope I won't be too late, Hedda, mm?

HEDDA: You'd better race up there . . .

(BERTE *comes in from the hall.*)

BERTE: Judge Brack is here, he wants to know if he can come in.

TESMAN: Now? No, I can't possibly see him now.

HEDDA: I can. (*To* BERTE.) Show him in.

(*Exit* BERTE.)

(*Whispering hurriedly*) Tesman, the parcel!

(*She snatches it up from the footstool.*)

TESMAN: Oh, yes, give it to me.

HEDDA: No, no, I'll look after it for you.

(*She goes over to the writing table and puts the parcel on the bookshelf.* TESMAN *is in a hurry and finding it impossible to get his gloves on.* BRACK *enters from the hall.*)

(*Nodding to him*) Well, you're an early bird, aren't you?

BRACK: Yes, I am, aren't I? (*To* TESMAN.) Off on your travels again?

TESMAN: Yes, I have to run up to my aunts'. One of them, the invalid, you know, poor thing, can you imagine, she's dying.

BRACK: Oh, my God, is she? You mustn't let me keep you, then. At a time like this . . .

64

TESMAN: Yes, I must dash, really . . . Goodbye, goodbye.
(*He hurries out through the hall door.*)

HEDDA: (*Approaching*) Well, Judge Brack, I gather things were more than lively at your party last night.

BRACK: I certainly haven't had time to undress, Hedda.

HEDDA: You as well?

BRACK: As you can see. What's Tesman been telling you about the night's dramas?

HEDDA: Oh, nothing remotely interesting. Just some story about them going and having coffee somewhere.

BRACK: Yes, I heard about the coffee party. I understand Eilert Lovborg wasn't with them?

HEDDA: No, they took him home before that.

BRACK: Tesman took him home?

HEDDA: No, he told me some of the others did.

BRACK: You know, Hedda, George Tesman really is a trusting soul.

HEDDA: Well, God knows that's true. Why, is there something more to all this?

BRACK: I must admit that there is.

HEDDA: Well! Let's sit down, shall we, Judge? Then you can tell me about it in comfort.
(*She sits at the left-hand end of the table,* BRACK *sits on the long side of the table, near her.*)
Carry on.

BRACK: I had special reasons for keeping track of my guests, or rather some of my guests, last night.

HEDDA: Was one of those by any chance Eilert Lovborg?

BRACK: I must confess that he was.

HEDDA: Now you're getting me really interested . . .

BRACK: Do you know where he and some of the others spent the rest of the night, Hedda?

HEDDA: If you feel you can tell me, I wish you would.

BRACK: Of course I can tell you. They finished up at a particularly interesting soirée.

HEDDA: Lively?

BRACK: Extremely lively.

HEDDA: You wouldn't like to enlarge on that, would you, Judge?

BRACK: In fact, Lovborg had been invited to it some time ago. As I very well knew. But at that time he had refused the invitation. Because, as you know, he has recently transformed himself.

HEDDA: You mean at the Elvsteds'? But even so, he went?

BRACK: Yes, well, you see, Hedda, last night, at my house, I'm afraid the spirit moved him.

HEDDA: Yes, I'm told he was quite inspired.

BRACK: Tremendously inspired. To the point of violence. And that, I suppose, led on to certain other thoughts. You see, unfortunately, we men, our principles are not always as firm as they ought to be.

HEDDA: Oh, I'm sure that doesn't apply to you, Judge Brack. But Lovborg, you were saying . . .

BRACK: Well, to cut a long story short . . . he finished up at Miss Diana's apartments.

HEDDA: Miss Diana?

BRACK: It was Miss Diana who was giving the soirée. For a select group of her friends and admirers.

HEDDA: Is she a redhead?

BRACK: That's right.

HEDDA: A kind of singer?

BRACK: Among other things, yes. Also, appropriately enough, a mighty huntress . . . of men, Hedda. I'm sure you must have heard of her. Eilert Lovborg was one of her most energetic supporters . . . in palmier days.

HEDDA: How did it all end?

BRACK: Not altogether cordially, it seems. Miss Diana welcomed him very enthusiastically, but it seems to have ended in fisticuffs.

HEDDA: Between her and Lovborg?

BRACK: Yes. He accused her or one of her friends of stealing from him. He insisted that his notebook had disappeared. As well as various other things. In fact, he seems to have started the most murderous row.

HEDDA: And what happened then?

BRACK: What happened then was a free-for-all, with women joining in as well as men. Eventually, I'm happy to say, the police arrived.

HEDDA: The police?

BRACK: Yes. It's going to be one of Eilert Lovborg's most expensive pranks. Lunatic.

HEDDA: Why do you say that?

BRACK: Apparently he resisted with some violence. Apparently he attacked one of the constables, beat him about the ears and ripped his tunic to pieces. After which, they asked him to accompany them to the station.

HEDDA: How did you find all this out?

BRACK: From the police.

HEDDA: (*Staring straight in front of her*) So that's what happened. No vine leaves in his hair.

BRACK: Vine leaves, Hedda?

HEDDA: (*Changing her tone*) Tell me, Judge . . . why are you so interested in keeping track of Eilert Lovborg?

BRACK: Well, in the first place, it would hardly be a matter of complete indifference to me if it were to come out in court that he'd come straight from my house.

HEDDA: There'll be a court case then, will there?

BRACK: Of course. Not that we really need to have any worries about that. No, what I thought was, that, as a friend of the family, it was my duty to keep you and Tesman fully informed about what he got up to last night.

HEDDA: But why, Judge Brack?

BRACK: Well, because I have a shrewd suspicion he's going to use you as a sort of refuge.

HEDDA: Whatever makes you think that?

BRACK: Good God, Hedda, we're not blind, now are we? You just wait and see. And Mrs Elvsted, she won't be leaving town in a hurry.

HEDDA: But . . . assuming there is something going on between those two, there are enough places they can meet besides here, aren't there?

BRACK: No. Nowhere. From now on, just as before, every

respectable house will be closed to Eilert Lovborg.

HEDDA: And you mean mine should be too?

BRACK: Yes. I must admit I would find it more than distressing if that man were to find sanctuary here. He'd be an intruder, a superfluous element, he would disrupt the . . . er . . .

HEDDA: The triangle?

BRACK: For me it would be as if I'd suddenly become homeless.

HEDDA: (*Looking at him and smiling*) So, you want to be the only bull in the pen, is that your aim?

BRACK: (*Nods slowly and lowers his voice*) Yes, that's my aim. And it's an aim I'll fight to achieve . . . with every means I have at my disposal.

HEDDA: (*As her smile fades*) I see when it comes to it you're a dangerous man.

BRACK: Do you think so?

HEDDA: Yes, I'm beginning to think so. I don't mind . . . as long as you never have any kind of hold over me.

BRACK: (*An ambiguous laugh*) Yes, you may be right, Hedda. If I did, who knows, I might want to take advantage of it.

HEDDA: Now, really, Judge Brack. That sounds almost like a threat.

BRACK: (*Standing up*) Not at all. No, my point is that the defence and protection of the triangle should be voluntary.

HEDDA: I agree with you.

BRACK: Well, now I've said what I came to say, I might as well be getting back to town. Goodbye, Hedda.
(*He moves towards the glass door.*)

HEDDA: (*Standing up*) Are you going out through the garden?

BRACK: Yes, it's a short cut for me.

HEDDA: Yes, and it's also the back way, isn't it?

BRACK: Very true. I have nothing against back ways. Sometimes they can be quite exciting.

HEDDA: You mean when there's shooting going on?

BRACK: (*In the doorway, laughing*) Surely no one would want to shoot at their tame bull.

HEDDA: (*Also laughing*) No, especially if it were the only one they had.

(*They nod and say goodbye, laughing. He leaves. She closes the door behind him.* HEDDA, *now quite serious, stands there for a moment, looking out. Then she goes over to the back wall and peeps through the curtains. She moves over to the writing table, takes Lovborg's parcel off the bookshelf and is about to look through the manuscript, when* BERTE'S *voice is heard loud in the hall.* HEDDA *stands and listens. Then she hurriedly pushes the parcel into a drawer, locks it and puts the key on the writing table.* LOVBORG, *still wearing his overcoat and carrying his hat, bursts through the hall door. He looks confused and upset.*)

LOVBORG: (*Turned towards the hall*) I've told you, I must go in and I will! And that's that.
(*He closes the door, turns round, sees* HEDDA, *regains his self-control immediately and bows.*)

HEDDA: (*At the writing table*) Ah, Mr Lovborg, you've come to collect Thea. Rather late, aren't you?

LOVBORG: You mean it's rather early to intrude on you. Please forgive me.

HEDDA: How do you know she's still here?

LOVBORG: They told me at her lodgings she'd been out all night.

HEDDA: (*Walking over to the drawing-room table*) Did you notice anything about them when they told you that?

LOVBORG: (*Looking inquiringly at her*) Notice anything?

HEDDA: I mean, did they seem to have any opinion on the matter?

LOVBORG: (*Suddenly understanding*) Oh, yes, of course, you mean what do they think about my dragging her down with me. I'm afraid I was in no condition to notice anything . . . I don't suppose Tesman is up yet.

HEDDA: No, I don't think so.

LOVBORG: When did he get home?

HEDDA: Very late.

LOVBORG: Did he say anything to you?

HEDDA: He told me it had all been very spirited at Judge Brack's.

LOVBORG: Is that all?

HEDDA: Yes, I think so. I was exhausted anyway.
(MRS ELVSTED *comes in from the back room.*)

MRS ELVSTED: (*Crossing to him*) Oh, Lovborg. At last!

LOVBORG: Yes, at last. And too late.

MRS ELVSTED: (*Looking at him anxiously*) What do you mean, too late?

LOVBORG: I mean, it's all too late now. I'm finished.

MRS ELVSTED: No, you aren't, don't say that.

LOVBORG: You'll say it as well, when I tell you what . . .

MRS ELVSTED: I don't want you to tell me anything!

HEDDA: Perhaps you'd like to speak to her alone? I'll leave you.

LOVBORG: No, you stay as well. I want you to stay, please.

MRS ELVSTED: I said I don't want you to tell me anything!

LOVBORG: It's not last night's adventures I want to talk to you about.

MRS ELVSTED: What is it, then?

LOVBORG: It's that, from now on, we're going to have to split up.

MRS ELVSTED: Split up?

HEDDA: (*Involuntarily*) I knew it!

LOVBORG: I don't need you any more, Thea.

MRS ELVSTED: How can you say that to me? You don't need me any more? I'm going to go on helping you, aren't I, as I used to? We're going to go on working together, aren't we?

LOVBORG: I've no intention of doing any more work.

MRS ELVSTED: (*In desperation*) Well, what do you expect me to do with my life?

LOVBORG: You must try to live the rest of your life as if you'd never met me.

MRS ELVSTED: I can't.

LOVBORG: You've got to try, Thea. You must go back home . . .

MRS ELVSTED: (*Protesting*) Never, I couldn't. I want to be wherever you are. I'm not going to let you send me away like that. I want to stay here with you. I want to be with you when your book comes out.

HEDDA: (*Half aloud, in suspense*) Oh, yes, the book . . .

LOVBORG: (*Looking at her*) My book and Thea's. That's what it is.

MRS ELVSTED: Yes, that's how I think of it. That's why it's my right to be with you when it comes out. I want to see you

70

respected again and showered with honours. And happy. I
want to share your happiness with you.

LOVBORG: Thea, our book will never come out.

HEDDA: Ah!

MRS ELVSTED: What do you mean?

LOVBORG: It can never come out.

MRS ELVSTED: (*A terrifying premonition*) Lovborg, what have you
done with the manuscript?

HEDDA: (*Looking at him anxiously*) The manuscript, yes . . . ?

MRS ELVSTED: Where is it?

LOVBORG: Thea, please don't ask me.

MRS ELVSTED: I will ask you, I want to know. I have a right to
know. Now.

LOVBORG: The manuscript . . . well, the thing is, I tore the
manuscript up into a thousand pieces.

MRS ELVSTED: (*Screaming*) No!

HEDDA: (*Involuntarily*) But that isn't . . . !

LOVBORG: (*Looking at her*) You don't think it's true?

HEDDA: (*Pulling herself together*) Well, obviously it is. If you say
so. It's just that it sounded so unlikely . . .

LOVBORG: All the same, it's true.

MRS ELVSTED: (*Wringing her hands*) Oh, God . . . Oh, God,
Hedda . . . all that work, he's torn it all to pieces!

LOVBORG: I've torn my life to pieces. Why shouldn't I tear up my
life's work as well . . . ?

MRS ELVSTED: And you did that last night?

LOVBORG: Yes. Yes, I did. Into a thousand pieces. Which I then
scattered into the fjord. A long way out. At least there there's
cool salt water. So they can drift. Drift with the current and
the wind. And after a while they can sink. Deeper and
deeper. Like me, Thea.

MRS ELVSTED: You know, Lovborg, what you've done with the
book . . . it's like . . . all my life I shall think of it as if you'd
killed a little child.

LOVBORG: That's right. Child murder.

MRS ELVSTED: But how could you? It was my child as well.

HEDDA: (*Almost inaudibly*) A child . . .

MRS ELVSTED: (*Sighing*) That's the end of it. Yes. I'm going now, Hedda.

HEDDA: You're not going to leave town, are you?

MRS ELVSTED: I don't know what I'm going to do. There's nothing but darkness ahead of me now.

(*She exits by the hall door.* HEDDA *stands waiting for a moment.*)

HEDDA: Aren't you going to see her home, Mr Lovborg?

LOVBORG: Me? Through the streets? Suppose people were to see her with me?

HEDDA: I don't know what else you did last night. Was it as irredeemable as that?

LOVBORG: Last night was only the beginning. I know that for sure. But the fact is, I can't even bring myself to go back to that kind of life. Not all over again. She's broken my courage and my spirit.

HEDDA: (*Staring in front of her*) That pretty little fool has dipped her fingers in a human destiny. (*Looks at him.*) Even so, I don't know how you could be so cruel to her.

LOVBORG: Don't say I was cruel.

HEDDA: To take something which had been her whole life and destroy it. Don't you think that was cruel?

LOVBORG: I can tell you the truth, Hedda.

HEDDA: The truth?

LOVBORG: Promise me first . . . swear to me that Thea will never find out what I'm about to tell you.

HEDDA: I swear.

LOVBORG: All right. It wasn't true what I told her just now.

HEDDA: About the manuscript?

LOVBORG: I didn't tear it up. Or throw it into the fjord.

HEDDA: Then . . . if you didn't . . . where is it?

LOVBORG: I've still destroyed it. Completely.

HEDDA: I don't understand.

LOVBORG: Thea said that, for her, what I'd done was like a child murder.

HEDDA: Yes . . .

LOVBORG: But to kill his child isn't the worst thing a father can do.

HEDDA: Isn't it?

LOVBORG: No. And I didn't want Thea to find out the worst.

HEDDA: What is the worst?

LOVBORG: Suppose that in the early hours of the morning, after a wild, drunken night out, a man were to come back to his child's mother and say, 'Listen, these are the places I've been. I've been there and there and there. And I took our child with me. There and there and there. And I've lost the child. Completely lost him. God knows who's got hold of him. Who's got their hands on him.'

HEDDA: But, I mean, when all's said and done, it was only a book.

LOVBORG: Thea's pure heart was in that book.

HEDDA: Yes, I understand.

LOVBORG: Then I expect you'll also understand that there can be no future for her and me.

HEDDA: So what are you going to do now?

LOVBORG: Nothing. Just finish it all. The sooner the better.

HEDDA: (*Moving a step nearer*) Eilert Lovborg, listen to me . . . Please make sure you . . . you do it beautifully.

LOVBORG: Beautifully? (*Smiles.*) With vine leaves in my hair, as you used to imagine me?

HEDDA: No, no. I don't believe in the vine leaves any more. But beautifully all the same. Just for once. Goodbye. You must go now. And never come here again.

LOVBORG: Goodbye, Mrs Tesman. Remember me to your husband.

(*He is about to leave.*)

HEDDA: No, wait. I want you to have a keepsake to remind you of me.

(*She crosses to the writing table and opens the pistol case. Then she returns to* LOVBORG, *bringing one of the pistols.*)

LOVBORG: (*Looking at her*) That? Is that the keepsake?

HEDDA: (*Nodding slowly*) Do you recognize it? It was aimed at you once.

LOVBORG: You should have used it then.

HEDDA: Take it. Use it now.

LOVBORG: (*Putting the pistol in his breast pocket*) Thank you.

73

HEDDA: And beautifully, Eilert Lovborg. Promise me!

LOVBORG: Goodbye, Hedda Gabler.

> (*He exits by the hall door.* HEDDA *listens at the door for a while. Then she goes over to the writing table, takes out the parcel of manuscript, glances under the wrapping, pulls a few of the sheets halfway out and looks at them. Then she takes it over and sits in the armchair by the stove. She puts the parcel in her lap. After a while, she opens the door of the stove, then the parcel.*)

HEDDA: (*Throwing a few pages of manuscript on to the fire and whispering*) I'm burning your child, Thea. Curly-haired Thea. (*Throws a few more pages into the stove.*) Your child and Eilert Lovborg's child. (*Throws the rest in.*) I'm burning it, I'm burning your child.

ACT FOUR

The Tesmans' room again. Evening. The drawing room is lit by the lamp which hangs over the table. The curtains are drawn in front of the glass door.

HEDDA, *dressed in black, is pacing up and down in the dark room. She goes into the back room and out of sight to the left. A few chords are played on the piano. Then she reappears and moves back into the drawing room.* BERTE *enters from the right through the back room, carrying a lighted lamp, which she puts on the table in front of the corner sofa in the living room. Her eyes are red from weeping and she has black ribbons in her cap. She exits left, quietly and discreetly.* HEDDA *crosses to the glass door, lifts the curtains a little and looks out into the night. A moment later,* MISS TESMAN, *dressed in mourning and wearing a hat with a veil, enters through the hall.* HEDDA *goes towards her and shakes hands with her.*

MISS TESMAN: You see me in the colours of mourning, Hedda. My poor sister has finally given up the struggle.

HEDDA: As you can see, I've already heard the news. Tesman sent me a card.

MISS TESMAN: Yes, he promised me he would. Even so, Hedda, I felt I should announce the death myself . . . here in the house of the living.

HEDDA: That was very kind of you.

MISS TESMAN: Ah, Rina should never have died now. This is no time for Hedda's house to be in mourning.

HEDDA: (*Changing the subject*) Miss Tesman died peacefully, did she?

MISS TESMAN: Yes, it ended very gently, very calmly. And she had the inexpressible happiness of seeing George again. And being able to say goodbye to him properly. Hasn't he come back yet?

HEDDA: No. He told me not to expect him back for a while. Won't you sit down?

75

MISS TESMAN: No, thank you, Hedda, my dear. I'd like to. But I don't have very much time. I have to lay her out and prepare her as well as I can. I want her to go to her grave looking really lovely.

HEDDA: Is there anything I can do to help?

MISS TESMAN: Of course not, you must put that out of your mind. We can't have Hedda Tesman turning her hand to that kind of work. Or her thoughts. Not now, not now.

HEDDA: It's not always possible to control one's thoughts.

MISS TESMAN: (*Continuing*) Oh, dear, oh, dear, that's the way the world goes. At home we're sewing Rina's shroud. And soon there'll be sewing here too, if I'm not mistaken. But of a different kind, thank God.

(TESMAN *enters by the hall door.*)

HEDDA: At last, I'm glad you're here.

TESMAN: You here, Auntie Julia? With Hedda? Well, well, well.

MISS TESMAN: My dear boy, I was just about to leave. Have you managed to do all the things you promised?

TESMAN: No, I'm afraid I must have forgotten at least half of them. I'll have to pop in and see you again tomorrow morning. I'm in a complete dither today. I can't concentrate.

MISS TESMAN: But, George dear, you mustn't take it like this.

TESMAN: What do you mean?

MISS TESMAN: You must feel happiness as well as grief. You must be happy about what has happened. I am.

TESMAN: Oh, you mean Auntie Rina.

HEDDA: You'll be lonely, won't you, Miss Tesman?

MISS TESMAN: At first, yes. But I'm hoping that won't last. I know poor Rina's room won't stay empty for very long.

TESMAN: Really? Who are you thinking of moving in then? Mm?

MISS TESMAN: Oh, well, it's a sad thing, but there's always some poor invalid needing care and attention.

HEDDA: Do you really want to take up that cross again?

MISS TESMAN: Cross? Good Lord, child, it's never seemed like a cross to me.

HEDDA: But surely a complete stranger . . .

MISS TESMAN: It doesn't take long to make friends with sick

people. And I need someone to live for as well, it's very important. And, thank God, an old aunt might be able to make herself useful soon, doing one or two things in this house.

HEDDA: Don't talk about us.

TESMAN: Just think what a lovely time the three of us could have together, if . . .

HEDDA: If what?

TESMAN: (*Uneasily*) Oh, never mind. Things will sort themselves out. Let's hope so, anyway. Mm?

MISS TESMAN: Well, I expect you have one or two things to discuss. (*Smiles.*) And I think perhaps Hedda may have something to say to you, George. Goodbye. I must be getting home to Rina. (*Turns at the door.*) Good Lord, I've just had the strangest thought. Do you realize that now Rina is with me and Jochum at the same time?

TESMAN: Yes, extraordinary, Auntie Julia, isn't it? Mm?
(*Exit* MISS TESMAN *by the hall door.*)

HEDDA: (*Following* TESMAN *with her eyes, coldly and searchingly*) I almost think the death has affected you more than it has her.

TESMAN: Oh, it's not only Auntie Rina. It's Eilert I'm really worried about.

HEDDA: (*Quickly*) Have you heard anything about him?

TESMAN: I ran over to see him this afternoon to tell him his manuscript was in safe hands.

HEDDA: And did you see him?

TESMAN: No. He wasn't there. But soon afterwards I met Mrs Elvsted and she told me he'd been here early this morning.

HEDDA: That's right, just after you left.

TESMAN: And apparently he said he'd torn his manuscript to pieces. Is that true? Mm?

HEDDA: So he maintained, yes.

TESMAN: Good God, he must have been completely out of his mind. I suppose you didn't dare give it back to him then, Hedda.

HEDDA: I didn't give it back to him, no.

TESMAN: But obviously you told him we had it.

HEDDA: No. (*Quickly*) Did you tell Mrs Elvsted?

TESMAN: No, I thought I'd better not. But you ought to have told him. He must be desperate about it, suppose he were to do himself an injury. Give me the manuscript, Hedda. I'd better run round with it straight away. Where've you put it?

HEDDA: (*Leaning on the armchair, cold and motionless*) I haven't got it.

TESMAN: You haven't got it? What do you mean, you haven't got it?

HEDDA: I burnt it. The whole thing.

TESMAN: (*Leaping up, horrified*) Burnt it? Burnt Eilert's manuscript?

HEDDA: Don't shout like that. The maid might hear you.

TESMAN: Burnt it? My God, no, you can't have done, it's impossible.

HEDDA: Nevertheless, that's what happened.

TESMAN: Do you realize what you've done, Hedda? It's illegal disposal of lost property. It's extraordinary. You ask Judge Brack, he'll tell you a few things.

HEDDA: I don't think it would be a very good idea to discuss it with Judge Brack . . . or, indeed, anyone.

TESMAN: But how could you do such a monstrous thing? How could you even think of it? What came over you? Mm? Answer me, mm?

HEDDA: (*Suppressing an almost imperceptible smile*) I did it for your sake, George.

TESMAN: For my sake?

HEDDA: When you came home this morning and told me he'd read to you . . .

TESMAN: Yes, yes, go on.

HEDDA: You said you'd envied him because of his book.

TESMAN: Yes, but I mean, I didn't mean it quite so literally.

HEDDA: Even so, I couldn't bear the thought that anyone should overshadow you.

TESMAN: (*An outburst of mixed doubt and joy*) Hedda . . . is that true? But I mean . . . but I mean . . . you've never shown your love like this before. It's extraordinary.

HEDDA: Yes, well, perhaps it's the best time for you to find out
about it . . . just when . . . (*Breaks off abruptly*.) No, you'd
better go and ask Aunt Julia. She'll tell you quick enough.

TESMAN: I think I understand you, Hedda, I think I do. (*Claps
his hands*.) Is it true, is it, mm?

HEDDA: Don't shout like that. The maid'll hear you.

TESMAN: (*Laughing, overjoyed*) The maid! I like that, Hedda, you
are priceless! The maid . . . Berte, you mean, you mean
Berte! I'll go and tell Berte myself.

HEDDA: (*Clenching her fists in desperation*) It's killing me, all this,
it's killing me.

TESMAN: What is, Hedda? Mm?

HEDDA: (*Cold, controlled*) It's all so . . . ridiculous . . . George.

TESMAN: Ridiculous? What's ridiculous about my being so
pleased and happy? Perhaps . . . perhaps I'd better not say
anything to Berte after all.

HEDDA: Oh, go on, why not tell her as well?

TESMAN: No. Not just yet. But I must certainly tell Auntie Julia.
I must tell her you've started calling me George, as well.
What about that, Auntie Julia will be so pleased, she'll be so
pleased.

HEDDA: When you tell her I burnt Eilert Lovborg's manuscript,
for your sake?

TESMAN: Oh, yes, that, well, of course, no one must know about
the manuscript. But your love for me, Hedda, I really must
tell Auntie Julia about that. I wonder if this kind of thing is
usual with newly-weds, what do you think? Mm?

HEDDA: You'd better ask Auntie Julia about that as well.

TESMAN: Yes, I will, I will, if I get the opportunity. (*Seems uneasy
and reflective again*.) As for the . . . er . . . the manuscript . . .
My God, it's terrible to think what's going to happen to
Eilert now.

(MRS ELVSTED, *dressed as she was at her first appearance,
wearing her hat and coat, enters by the hall door*.)

MRS ELVSTED: (*Acknowledging them hastily and speaking
agitatedly*) Oh, Hedda, don't be angry with me for coming
back.

HEDDA: What's the matter with you, Thea?

TESMAN: Is it something about Eilert Lovborg? Mm?

MRS ELVSTED: Yes, I'm terribly afraid he's had some accident.

HEDDA: (*Catching hold of her arm*) Do you think so?

TESMAN: Yes, but, I mean, what makes you think that, Mrs Elvsted?

MRS ELVSTED: I heard them talking about him at the boarding house . . . just as I came in. The most incredible rumours about him have been going around all day.

TESMAN: Yes, I've been hearing them as well, can you imagine? And I know he went straight home to bed last night, I'm a witness. It's extraordinary.

HEDDA: What were they saying at the boarding house?

MRS ELVSTED: I found nothing out. Either because they didn't know anything very definite, or because . . . They stopped talking as soon as they saw me. And I didn't dare ask.

TESMAN: (*Moving around uneasily*) Well, let's . . . let's hope you misunderstood them, Mrs Elvsted.

MRS ELVSTED: No, I'm convinced it was him they were talking about. And I heard them say something about the hospital and . . .

TESMAN: The hospital?

HEDDA: No, that's impossible.

MRS ELVSTED: I got desperately frightened. So I went up to his lodgings and asked them about him.

HEDDA: How could you bring yourself to do that?

MRS ELVSTED: What else could I have done? I felt I couldn't stand the uncertainty any longer.

TESMAN: And I suppose you didn't find him there either? Mm?

MRS ELVSTED: No. And the people there knew nothing about him. They said he hadn't been back there since yesterday afternoon.

TESMAN: Yesterday afternoon? But that's impossible.

MRS ELVSTED: So I'm sure something awful must have happened to him.

TESMAN: Hedda, perhaps I should go into town and make a few inquiries . . .

HEDDA: No, no, there's no need for you to get mixed up in this.
  (JUDGE BRACK, *carrying his hat, comes in through the hall door,
  shown in by* BERTE. *He looks very serious and bows silently.*)
TESMAN: Ah, Judge, it's you, is it? Mm?
BRACK: Yes, I felt I had to come and see you this evening.
TESMAN: I can see by your face you've heard the news from
  Auntie Julia.
BRACK: I've heard about that as well, yes.
TESMAN: Tragic, isn't it? Mm?
BRACK: Well, my dear Tesman, it depends how you look at it.
TESMAN: (*Looking at him uncertainly*) Is there something else as
  well?
BRACK: Yes. There is.
HEDDA: (*Tensely*) Something tragic, Judge Brack?
BRACK: Once again, it depends how you look at it, Mrs Tesman.
MRS ELVSTED: (*An involuntary outburst*) It's something to do with
  Eilert Lovborg!
BRACK: (*Glancing at her*) Whatever makes you think that, Mrs
  Elvsted? Unless, of course, you've heard about it
  already . . . ?
MRS ELVSTED: (*Confused*) No, I haven't, no, it's just . . .
TESMAN: For goodness' sake, tell us!
BRACK: (*Shrugging his shoulders*) Well, I'm sorry to say, Eilert
  Lovborg has been taken to hospital. He's dying.
MRS ELVSTED: (*Screaming*) Oh, God, oh, my God . . . !
TESMAN: Taken to hospital? Dying?
HEDDA: (*Involuntarily*) So soon . . .
MRS ELVSTED: (*Moaning*) And we separated without making it
  up, Hedda!
HEDDA: (*Whispering*) Thea, really, Thea!
MRS ELVSTED: (*Taking no notice*) I must go to him! I must see
  him alive!
BRACK: It's no use, Mrs Elvsted. No one's allowed to see him.
MRS ELVSTED: Can't you just tell me what's happened to him?
  How did it happen?
TESMAN: He hasn't . . . erm . . . er, has he? Mm?
HEDDA: Yes, I'm sure he has.

TESMAN: Hedda, how could you . . . ?

BRACK: (*Who has been watching her all the time*) I'm afraid you've guessed right, Mrs Tesman.

MRS ELVSTED: How terrible!

TESMAN: You mean he has? Extraordinary.

HEDDA: Shot himself.

BRACK: Right again, Mrs Tesman.

MRS ELVSTED: (*Trying to control herself*) When did it happen, Judge?

BRACK: This afternoon. Between three and four.

TESMAN: Oh, my God, where was he when he did it? Mm?

BRACK: (*Slightly thrown*) Where? He . . . er . . . I suppose at his lodgings.

MRS ELVSTED: No, he can't have been. I was there between six and seven.

BRACK: Well, somewhere else, then. I'm not sure. I only know he was found . . . He'd shot himself in the chest.

MRS ELVSTED: It's horrible to think of him dying like that!

HEDDA: (*To* BRACK) In the chest, did you say?

BRACK: I did, yes.

HEDDA: Not in the temple?

BRACK: In the chest, Mrs Tesman.

HEDDA: Yes, well . . . that will do.

BRACK: What do you mean?

HEDDA: (*Evasively*) Oh, nothing, nothing.

TESMAN: And you say the wound is dangerous, is it? Mm?

BRACK: Yes, absolutely fatal. It's probably all over already.

MRS ELVSTED: It is, I know it is! It's all over. All over. Oh, Hedda!

TESMAN: But tell me . . . how did you find out all this?

BRACK: (*Shortly*) From someone in the police. A man I was talking to.

HEDDA: (*Penetratingly*) At last, an achievement!

TESMAN: (*Shocked*) Good heavens, Hedda, what are you saying?

HEDDA: I'm saying, there's something beautiful about it.

BRACK: Mrs Tesman . . .

TESMAN: What do you mean, beautiful? Extraordinary thing to say.

MRS ELVSTED: Oh, Hedda, how can you talk about beauty after what's happened?

HEDDA: Eilert Lovborg has had a reckoning with himself. He has had the courage to do what . . . what had to be done.

MRS ELVSTED: You mustn't think it happened like that, it didn't. What he did was an act of despair.

TESMAN: An act of total despair, that's what it was.

HEDDA: No, it wasn't. I'm sure it wasn't.

MRS ELVSTED: It was! Despair. Like when he tore up our book.

BRACK: (*Puzzled*) Book? Do you mean his manuscript? Did he tear that up?

MRS ELVSTED: Yes, last night.

TESMAN: (*Whispering softly*) Oh, Hedda, we're never going to get away with this.

BRACK: Really, that's very curious.

TESMAN: (*Crossing the room*) It's terrible to think of Eilert passing on like this. Without leaving behind the thing that would have immortalized his name . . .

MRS ELVSTED: If only it could be pieced together again . . .

TESMAN: Yes, if only it could! I don't know what I wouldn't give to . . .

MRS ELVSTED: Perhaps it could, Mr Tesman.

TESMAN: What do you mean?

MRS ELVSTED: (*Searching in her handbag*) Look. I've kept all these loose scraps of paper he used to have with him when he dictated.

HEDDA: (*Moving a step nearer*) Ah!

TESMAN: You kept them, did you, Mrs Elvsted? Mm?

MRS ELVSTED: Yes, here they are. I brought them with me when I came. And they've been lying in my bag ever since . . .

TESMAN: Let's have a look!

MRS ELVSTED: (*Passing him a handful of scraps of paper*) But they're not in any order. They're completely mixed up.

TESMAN: Can you imagine, if we could work it out anyway? Perhaps if we helped each other . . .

MRS ELVSTED: Oh, yes, let's at least try it . . .

TESMAN: It will work. It's got to work! I'll devote my life to it.

HEDDA: Your life, George?

TESMAN: Yes, well, I mean, all the time I can spare. I'll put aside
my own research for a while. Do you understand me,
Hedda? Mm? I owe it to Eilert's memory.

HEDDA: Possibly.

TESMAN: Well, Mrs Elvsted, let's pull ourselves together, shall
we? I mean, good Lord, there's no sense in brooding about
what's already happened, is there? Mm? We must do our
best to find sufficient peace of mind to . . .

MRS ELVSTED: Yes, Mr Tesman, I'll try as hard as I can.

TESMAN: Well, come on then. Let's have a look at these notes
right away. Where shall we sit? Here? No, let's go in the
back room. Would you excuse me, Judge? Come along, Mrs
Elvsted.

MRS ELVSTED: Oh, God, if only it were possible.

(TESMAN *and* MRS ELVSTED *go into the back room. She takes
off her hat and overcoat. They sit at the table, under the hanging
lamp, and are soon engrossed in searching eagerly through the
papers.* HEDDA *crosses to the stove and sits in the armchair. A
moment later* BRACK *joins her.*)

HEDDA: (*Half aloud*) Oh, Judge, there's such a sense of release in
what Eilert Lovborg's done.

BRACK: Release? Well, it was certainly a release for him . . .

HEDDA: I meant for me. It's a release to know that in spite of
everything a premeditated act of courage is still possible.
Something with at least some spark of instinctive beauty.

BRACK: (*Smiling*) Well, Hedda . . .

HEDDA: Oh, I know what you're going to say. You're a kind of
academic, too, aren't you, like . . . aren't you?

BRACK: (*Watching her closely*) Eilert Lovborg meant more to you
than you perhaps want to admit, even to yourself. Or am I
quite mistaken?

HEDDA: I'm not going to answer questions like that. All I know is
that Eilert Lovborg had the courage to live his life the way he
wanted to live it. To its final great and beautiful
achievement. When he had the strength and willpower to
walk out on life . . . early.

BRACK: It grieves me, Hedda . . . but I'm afraid I'm going to have to shatter an agreeable illusion.

HEDDA: Illusion?

BRACK: Which couldn't have lasted long in any case.

HEDDA: What do you mean?

BRACK: His shooting himself. It wasn't . . . premeditated.

HEDDA: Wasn't premeditated?

BRACK: No. What I said about Eilert wasn't entirely accurate.

HEDDA: (*In suspense*) Have you kept something back? What?

BRACK: For the sake of poor Mrs Elvsted, I felt it necessary to employ a few little euphemisms.

HEDDA: Go on.

BRACK: Well, in the first place, he's already dead.

HEDDA: At the hospital?

BRACK: Yes. He died without regaining consciousness.

HEDDA: What else?

BRACK: It . . . er . . . didn't happen in his room.

HEDDA: Well, I don't see that that matters very much.

BRACK: I think it may. You see, I might as well tell you, Eilert Lovborg was found shot in . . . Miss Diana's . . . boudoir.

HEDDA: (*Starting to jump up, then sinking back*) But that's impossible. He can't have been round there again today.

BRACK: He went round there this afternoon. He went to demand something he said they'd taken from him. Told some incomprehensible story about a lost child . . .

HEDDA: Oh, that's it . . .

BRACK: I thought he might have been talking about his manuscript. But now I'm told he destroyed that himself. Perhaps he meant his notebook.

HEDDA: Yes, he must have done. So . . . so he was found there?

BRACK: Yes. With an empty pistol in his inside pocket. And a fatal wound.

HEDDA: In the chest . . .

BRACK: No . . . somewhat lower.

HEDDA: (*Looks up at him with an expression of disgust*) It's like some curse, everything I touch turns into something ludicrous and disgusting.

BRACK: There's another thing, Hedda. Another unpleasant aspect of the case.

HEDDA: What?

BRACK: The pistol he had with him . . .

HEDDA: (*Breathlessly*) What about it?

BRACK: Must have been stolen.

HEDDA: (*Jumping up*) Stolen? That's not true! It wasn't!

BRACK: It's the only possible explanation. He must have stolen it . . . Ssh!

(TESMAN *and* MRS ELVSTED *have risen from the table in the back room and move into the drawing room.*)

TESMAN: (*Hands full of papers*) Listen, Hedda, it's almost impossible for me to see anything under that lamp, can you imagine?

HEDDA: Yes, I can imagine.

TESMAN: Might we be allowed to sit at your writing table for a bit? Mm?

HEDDA: Yes, all right. (*Quickly*) No, wait a minute! Let me clear it first.

TESMAN: There's no need to, Hedda. There's plenty of room.

HEDDA: I said, let me clear it. I'll just put these things on the piano for the time being. There we are.

(*She has pulled something out from under the bookshelf, invisible under sheet music, piles some more sheet music on top of it and moves to the left, carrying the whole lot into the back room.*

TESMAN *puts his papers on the writing table and moves the lamp over from the corner table. He and* MRS ELVSTED *sit down and start working again.* HEDDA *returns.*)

(*Behind* MRS ELVSTED'*s chair, running her fingers through her hair*) Dear Thea . . . how's it going with Eilert Lovborg's memorial?

MRS ELVSTED: (*Looking at her, somewhat dispirited*) It's going to be terribly difficult sorting it all out.

TESMAN: It's got to work. There's no alternative. Anyway, sorting out, collating other people's papers is exactly what I'm best at.

(HEDDA *crosses the room and sits on one of the stools.* BRACK *stands over her, leaning against the armchair.*)

HEDDA: (*Whispering*) What were you saying about the pistol?

BRACK: (*Quietly*) That he must have stolen it.

HEDDA: Why should he have stolen it?

BRACK: It's the only possible explanation, Hedda.

HEDDA: Is it?

BRACK: (*Glancing at her*) Eilert Lovborg was here this morning, wasn't he?

HEDDA: Yes.

BRACK: Were you alone with him?

HEDDA: Yes, for a bit.

BRACK: You didn't leave the room while he was here?

HEDDA: No.

BRACK: Are you sure? Not even for a minute?

HEDDA: Well, perhaps just for a minute, when I went out to the hall.

BRACK: And where was your pistol case this morning?

HEDDA: Locked in the . . .

BRACK: Really, Hedda?

HEDDA: No, over there on the writing table.

BRACK: And have you checked to see if both pistols are still there?

HEDDA: No.

BRACK: You needn't bother. I saw the pistol Lovborg had on him. I recognized it immediately as one I'd seen yesterday. And on previous occasions.

HEDDA: Have you got it?

BRACK: No, the police have got it.

HEDDA: What will the police do with it?

BRACK: Try to track down its owner.

HEDDA: Do you think they'll succeed?

BRACK: (*Bending over and whispering*) No, Hedda Gabler, as long as I don't say anything.

HEDDA: (*Looking up at him, frightened*) And what if you do say something?

BRACK: (*Shrugging his shoulders*) You could always tell them the pistol was stolen.

HEDDA: (*Firmly*) I'd rather die.

BRACK: (*Smiling*) People say things like that. But they never do them.

HEDDA: (*Without answering*) And suppose the pistol wasn't stolen? And they find the owner? What then?

BRACK: Then, Hedda, I expect there would be a scandal.

HEDDA: A scandal?

BRACK: Yes, the kind of scandal you're so terribly afraid of. You'd have to go to court, of course. You and Miss Diana. She'll have to explain how it happened. Whether it was an accident or murder. Was he trying to take the pistol out of his pocket to threaten her, when it suddenly went off? Or did she wrench the pistol out of his hand, shoot him and put it back in his pocket? That would be quite like her. She's quite a beefy young lady, Miss Diana.

HEDDA: But all that vile business has got nothing to do with me.

BRACK: No. You'll just have to answer one question: why did you give Eilert Lovborg the pistol? And when it comes out that you did give it to him, what inevitable conclusions do you suppose people will jump to?

HEDDA: (*Her head sinking*) I see. I hadn't thought of that.

BRACK: Fortunately, of course, as long as I keep quiet about it, there's no danger.

HEDDA: (*Looking up at him*) So, I am in your power, am I, Judge? From now on you do have a hold over me.

BRACK: (*Whispering softly*) Dearest Hedda . . . believe me . . . I shan't take advantage of my position.

HEDDA: I'll still be in your power. Dependent on your demands and whims. A slave. I'll be a slave. (*Gets up quickly.*) No, I can't bear the thought of it! I can't!

BRACK: (*Looking at her, half scornfully*) As a rule, one comes to accept the inevitable.

HEDDA: (*Returning his gaze*) Possibly. (*Crosses to the writing table. Suppressing an involuntary smile and imitating* TESMAN's *intonation.*) Well? How are you getting on, George? Mm?

TESMAN: God knows. There's months of work here, months, at least.

HEDDA: (*As before*) Extraordinary. (*Runs her fingers through* MRS

ELVSTED's *hair*.) Don't you find it strange, Thea? Sitting here with Tesman, as you used to sit with Eilert Lovborg?

MRS ELVSTED: If only I could inspire your husband in the same way.

HEDDA: I'm sure you will. Given time.

TESMAN: It's a funny thing, Hedda, but I really think something of the sort is beginning to happen. Now, go and sit down and talk to the Judge again.

HEDDA: Is there nothing I can do to make myself useful?

TESMAN: No, not a thing. (*Turns his head*.) Can I leave Hedda for you to look after from now on, Judge?

BRACK: (*Glancing at* HEDDA) Of course, with the greatest of pleasure.

HEDDA: Thank you. I'm tired this evening. I think I'll go and lie down on the sofa in there for a bit.

TESMAN: Yes, why don't you, dear? Mm?

(HEDDA *goes into the back room, drawing the curtains behind her. A brief pause. Suddenly she is heard playing a wild dance tune on the piano*.)

MRS ELVSTED: (*Jumping up from her chair*) Ah . . . what's that?

TESMAN: (*Running over to the doorway*) Please, Hedda dear, I don't think dance music is very appropriate this evening. What about Auntie Rina? And Eilert?

HEDDA: (*Putting her head out between the curtains*) And Auntie Julia. And all the rest of them . . . From now on I'm not going to make any more noise.

(*She closes the curtains again*.)

TESMAN: (*At the writing table*) It's not good for her, you know, seeing us doing this melancholy work. I tell you what, Mrs Elvsted, why don't you move in with my Auntie Julia? Then I could come up in the evenings. And we could sit and work there, couldn't we? Mm?

MRS ELVSTED: Well, that might be an idea . . .

HEDDA: (*From the back room*) I can hear what you're saying, Tesman. How do you suppose I'm going to while away my evenings here?

TESMAN: (*Looking through the papers*) I'm sure Judge Brack will be kind enough to come over and see you, even if I'm not here.

BRACK: (*Calling out happily from the armchair*) Every evening, Mrs Tesman, without fail. I'm sure the two of us will have a really enjoyable time together.

HEDDA: (*Loud and clear*) That's what you're hoping for, isn't it, Judge? Now you're the only bull in the pen . . .

(*A shot rings out from within.* TESMAN, MRS ELVSTED *and* BRACK *leap to their feet.*)

TESMAN: I suppose she's playing with those pistols again.

(*He throws back the curtains and hurries in, followed by* MRS ELVSTED. HEDDA *is lying dead, stretched out on the sofa. Confusion and cries.* BERTE *comes rushing in from the right.*) (*Shouting at* BRACK) She's shot herself! She's shot herself in the head! Extraordinary!

BRACK: (*Half helpless in the armchair*) What do you mean, my God, people don't do things like that!

A DOLL'S HOUSE

CHARACTERS

TORVALD HELMER
NORA
DR RANK
MRS KRISTINE LINDE
NILS KROGSTAD
ANNE-MARIE
MAID (Helene)
THE HELMERS' CHILDREN
ERRAND BOY

The action takes place in the Helmers' flat.

ACT ONE   Christmas Eve
ACT TWO   Christmas Day
ACT THREE   The day after Christmas

Christopher Hampton's adaptation of Henrik Ibsen's *A Doll's House*, from a literal translation by Hélène Grégoire, was first performed at the Playhouse Theatre, New York.

The cast was as follows:

TORVALD HELMER	Donald Madden
NORA	Claire Bloom
DR RANK	Roy Shuman
MRS KRISTINE LINDE	Patricia Elliott
NILS KROGSTAD	Robert Gerringer
ANNE-MARIE	Kate Wilkinson
HELENE	Eda Reiss Merin
THE HELMERS' CHILDREN	Michael Calvet
	Jill Grafflin
Director	Patrick Garland
Sets, Costumes, Lighting	John Bury
Producer	Hillard Elkins

It was later revived at the Riverside Studio, London, on
12 September 1988.
The cast was as follows:

TORVALD HELMER	Eamon Boland
NORA	Anna Carteret
DR RANK	Bill Wallis
MRS KRISTINE LINDE	Kate Fahy
NILS KROGSTAD	David Hargreaves
ANNE-MARIE	Barbara Keogh
HELENE	Tamar Thomas
THE HELMERS' CHILDREN	Oliver, Rupert and Miranda Bruton, Louise Penfold, Benjamin Brazier, Peter Warren
Director	Jan Sargent
Lighting	Leonard Tucker
Assistant Director	Chris Stanton
Decor	Stephanie Howard
Choreography	Trevor Hacker

ACT ONE

A comfortable room, tastefully but not expensively furnished. Upstage right, a door leading into the hall, upstage left, a door leading to Helmer's study. Between the two doors, a grand piano. In the middle of the left-hand wall, another door and, further forward, a window. Near the window, a round table with armchairs and a small sofa. Towards the back of the right-hand wall, a door and, further forward, a porcelain stove, two armchairs and a rocking chair, grouped round it. Between the stove and the side door, a small table. Engravings on the walls. Shelves with china and small objets d'art. A small bookcase filled with beautifully bound books. Carpet on the floor, fire in the stove. Winter day.

The doorbell rings out in the hall. Then, the front door opens. NORA enters, humming cheerfully. She is wearing an overcoat and carrying a pile of parcels which she puts down on the right-hand table. She leaves the door open behind her, revealing an ERRAND BOY, carrying a Christmas tree, and a basket, which he gives to the MAID who has opened the door for them.

NORA: Find a good hiding place for the Christmas tree, Helene. I don't want the children to see it till it's lit up this evening.
(*To the* ERRAND BOY, *opening her purse.*) How much do I owe you?
ERRAND BOY: Fifty ore.
NORA: Here you are. No, no, keep the change.
(*The* ERRAND BOY *thanks her and leaves.* NORA *closes the door. She takes a bag of macaroons out of her pocket and eats one or two, tiptoeing over towards the door of her husband's study and listening outside.*)
Yes, he's in.
(*She moves over to the table on the right, humming.*)
HELMER: (*Calling from the study*) Who's that chirping out there? Is it my little lark?
NORA: (*Busy opening the parcels*) It is.

97

HELMER: Is it that squirrel rummaging about again?

NORA: Yes.

HELMER: And when did my squirrel get home?

NORA: Just this minute. (*She puts the bag of macaroons in her pocket and wipes her mouth.*) If you come out, Torvald, I'll show you what I've bought.

HELMER: Do not disturb! (*A moment later, he opens the door and looks in, pen in hand.*) Did you say bought? What, all those things? Has my little prodigal been out frittering away all my money?

NORA: Oh, Torvald, surely this year we can let ourselves go a little. It's the first Christmas we haven't had to pinch and scrape.

HELMER: That doesn't mean we can go throwing money around.

NORA: I know, Torvald, but we can throw a bit around. Can't we? Just a teeny-weeny little bit. Soon you'll be getting an enormous salary and you'll have piles and piles of money.

HELMER: Yes, but not until the New Year. And then I don't get paid until the end of the first quarter.

NORA: Well, that doesn't matter, we can always borrow some.

HELMER: Nora! (*He moves over to the table and takes her playfully by the ear.*) What a scatterbrain you are. Suppose I were to borrow a thousand kroner today, and you were to fritter it away over Christmas. And then suppose on New Year's Eve a tile were to come off the roof and land on my head and kill me . . .

NORA: (*Putting her hand over his mouth*) Ssh, you mustn't say horrible things like that.

HELMER: Well, suppose something like that happened. Then where would you be?

NORA: If anything as awful as that happened, it wouldn't make any difference whether I had debts or not.

HELMER: But what about the people I'd borrowed from?

NORA: Who cares about them? They're strangers.

HELMER: Nora, Nora. That's just typical of a woman. No, but seriously, Nora, you know what I think about that sort of thing. Neither a borrower nor a lender be! There's no freedom in a house that's built on borrowing and debt, it becomes ugly. So far we've put up with everything bravely, both of us; and there's only a short time left, so we're not going to give up now.

NORA: (*Moving over to the stove*) All right, Torvald, just as you like.

HELMER: (*Following her*) Oh, now, that can't be my little skylark with her wings all drooping, can it? Mm? Is it a little sulking squirrel? (*Takes out his wallet.*) Nora, what's this then, eh?

NORA: (*Spinning round*) Money!

HELMER: That's right. (*Gives her some notes.*) I know you need all sorts of things round the house at Christmas.

NORA: (*Counting it*) Ten . . . twenty . . . thirty . . . forty. Oh, thank you, Torvald, thank you, that'll go a long way.

HELMER: I should certainly hope so.

NORA: Yes, it will, it will. Come here and let me show you what I've bought. Everything was so cheap! Look, this is a new suit for Ivar – and a toy sword. I got a horse and a trumpet for Bob. And a doll and a doll's cradle for Emmy; they're very ordinary – but she always breaks things so quickly, doesn't she? And some material and handkerchiefs for the servants. I really ought to have got something better than that for old Anne-Marie.

HELMER: And what's in that parcel?

NORA: (*Crying out*) Oh, no, Torvald, you mustn't look at that till this evening!

HELMER: Aha. I see. Now tell me, what does little moneybags want for herself?

NORA: For me? Oh, nothing, I don't really want anything.

HELMER: Of course you do. Go on, think of something you'd really like, something sensible.

NORA: No, really, I don't want anything. Except, Torvald . . .

HELMER: Yes?

NORA: (*Fiddling with his buttons, not looking at him*) Well, if you want to give me something, you could always . . . I mean, you could . . .

HELMER: Come on, out with it.

NORA: (*Quickly*) You could give me money, Torvald. Just what you thought you could afford, no more. Then I could buy myself something later.

HELMER: But, Nora . . .

NORA: Oh, do, Torvald dear, please, please do. Then I could wrap the money in lovely gold paper and hang it on the tree. That'd be fun, wouldn't it?

HELMER: What do I call those little birds who squander all their money away?

NORA: Spendswifts, Torvald, I know. But if we do what I suggest, I'll have time to think about what I need most. Doesn't that sound reasonable? Mm?

HELMER: (*Smiling*) Of course, it *sounds* reasonable. I mean, if you could really hold on to the money I gave you and really buy yourself something with it. But it'll just go on the housekeeping and all sorts of useless things, and then I'll have to fork out some more.

NORA: But, Torvald . . .

HELMER: You can't deny it, Nora darling. (*Puts his arms round her waist.*) Spendswifts are very sweet, but they get through an awful lot of money. It's incredible how expensive it can be to keep a little spendswift.

NORA: That's not fair, how can you say that? I save as much as I can.

HELMER: (*Laughing*) Of course you do. As much as you can. But as much as you can comes to nothing.

NORA: (*Humming and smiling, quietly happy*) Larks and squirrels always have lots and lots of expenses, Torvald, you can't imagine.

HELMER: You're a funny little thing. Just like your father. You're always on the look-out for all the money you can get your hands on. But as soon as you do get hold of some, it seems to slip away through your fingers, and you can never remember what you've done with it. Ah, well, I shall just have to accept you as you are. It's in the blood. Yes, Nora. Hereditary.

NORA: I wish I'd inherited a few more of Father's qualities.

HELMER: And I wouldn't wish you any different, you're my

sweet little skylark. Except . . . it seems to me you're looking a bit, erm, how shall I put it, a bit suspicious today . . .

NORA: Am I?

HELMER: Yes, you are. Look me straight in the eye.

NORA: (*Looking at him*) Yes?

HELMER: (*Wagging his finger*) Now, Miss Sweet-tooth, are you quite sure you didn't get up to anything in town today?

NORA: No, whatever makes you think that?

HELMER: Well, little Miss Sweet-tooth used to be forever popping round to the confectioner's.

NORA: No, I promise you, Torvald . . .

HELMER: Not even to nibble a little something with jam in it?

NORA: No, nothing.

HELMER: Not even to munch a macaroon or two?

NORA: No, really, Torvald. I promise you . . .

HELMER: It's all right, just my little joke . . .

NORA: (*Moving across to the table on the right*) I wouldn't dream of doing anything you disapproved of.

HELMER: No, I know that. And anyway, you promised, didn't you? (*Goes over to her.*) My dear Nora, you keep your little Christmas secrets to yourself. And they'll all be revealed this evening when the Christmas tree's lit up, won't they?

NORA: Did you remember to invite Dr Rank?

HELMER: No, it's not necessary. I'm sure he'll come to dinner of his own accord. Anyway, I can always ask him when he comes round this morning. I've ordered some very good wine. You can't imagine how much I'm looking forward to this evening, Nora.

NORA: I am too. And won't the children enjoy themselves, Torvald?

HELMER: Ah, it's marvellous to know one has a really solid, secure position. And such a comfortable income. It's a delightful thought, isn't it?

NORA: Wonderful.

HELMER: Remember last Christmas? How you shut yourself up till long after midnight every evening for three whole weeks, making flowers for the Christmas tree and all sorts of other

wonders you were going to amaze us with. Ha, I've never
been so bored in my life.

NORA: I wasn't at all bored.

HELMER: (*Smiling*) Didn't come to much, though, did it, Nora?

NORA: Oh, you're not going to tease me about that again, are
you? It wasn't my fault the cat got in and ripped everything
to pieces.

HELMER: Poor Nora, no, of course it wasn't. You wanted to give
us all a bit of pleasure and you did your best to, that's what
counts. All the same, it's a good thing the lean times are
over.

NORA: It's wonderful.

HELMER: Now I don't have to sit here on my own dying of
boredom, and you don't have to wear out your lovely eyes
and your dear little delicate hands . . .

NORA: (*Clapping her hands*) No, I don't, Torvald, do I? Isn't that
a wonderful thought? (*Takes his arm.*) Now, Torvald, I'll tell
you what I think we should do. As soon as Christmas is over,
I . . .

(*A ring at the doorbell.*)

Oh, that's the bell. (*Starts tidying up the room.*) It must be
someone come to call. That's rather a bore.

HELMER: I'm not at home. Don't forget.

MAID: (*In the doorway*) Madam, there's a lady here to see you, no
one I know.

NORA: Show her in.

MAID: (*To* HELMER) The doctor's here as well.

HELMER: Has he gone into the study?

MAID: Yes.

(HELMER *goes into his study. The* MAID *shows in* MRS LINDE,
who is wearing travelling clothes, and shuts the door behind her.)

MRS LINDE: (*Nervous and hesitant*) Good morning, Nora.

NORA: (*Uncertainly*) Good morning . . .

MRS LINDE: You don't recognize me, do you?

NORA: No, I don't think I do. Oh yes, of course I do . . .
(*Expansively*) Kristine! Is it really you?

MRS LINDE: Yes, it is.

NORA: Kristine! Fancy me not recognizing you. But how could I, you . . . (*More gently*) You've changed so much, Kristine.

MRS LINDE: Yes, I must have. In nine . . . ten years, it's a long time . . .

NORA: Is it as long as that since we met? Yes, it must be. I've been so happy these last eight years, you know. So have you moved into town as well? All that long journey in the winter. That was very brave.

MRS LINDE: I arrived this morning, by boat.

NORA: You must have come up to spend Christmas here. How lovely! We'll all have a much happier Christmas now. Do take your coat off. Are you freezing? (*Helps her.*) Come over here by the fire and sit down. No, take the armchair. And I'll sit in the rocking chair. (*She takes her hands.*) Now, you look the same as ever. It was just when I first saw you . . . You look a bit paler, Kristine . . . and perhaps a bit thinner.

MRS LINDE: And much older, Nora, much, much older.

NORA: Perhaps a little bit older. But only a teeny-weeny bit. Certainly not much. (*Stops suddenly; then, seriously*) Oh, I'm so thoughtless, sitting here, prattling on. Forgive me, Kristine, please, can you?

MRS LINDE: What do you mean, Nora?

NORA: (*Gently*) Poor Kristine, you're a widow now, aren't you?

MRS LINDE: Yes, I have been for three years.

NORA: Yes, I know, I saw it in the paper. Oh, you must believe me, Kristine, I kept meaning to write to you. But I was always putting it off and having to do something else.

MRS LINDE: That's all right, Nora, I understand.

NORA: No, it was terrible of me, Kristine. What you must have gone through, you poor thing. Did he leave you anything to live on?

MRS LINDE: No.

NORA: No children?

MRS LINDE: No.

NORA: Nothing at all?

MRS LINDE: Not even grief, not even a lingering regret.

NORA: (*Looking at her incredulously*) But how can that be, Kristine?

MRS LINDE: (*Smiling and stroking her hair*) Oh, that's the way things are sometimes, Nora.

NORA: All alone. That must be terribly hard for you. I've got three lovely children. I can't show them to you now, they're out with their nanny. But now you must tell me all about yourself.

MRS LINDE: No, no, it's better if you do the talking.

NORA: No, you start. I mustn't be selfish today. Today I just want to think about you. Except there is one thing I must tell you. Have you heard about our great stroke of luck?

MRS LINDE: No, what's that?

NORA: Just think, my husband's been made manager of the Joint Stock Bank.

MRS LINDE: Your husband? Isn't that marvellous!

NORA: Yes, extraordinary! You see, being a lawyer is such an insecure life, especially if you don't want to get involved in anything dishonest and underhand. Which of course Torvald didn't. And I absolutely agree with him. So you can imagine how pleased we are! He'll be starting at the bank in the New Year, and he'll be earning a large salary and quite a lot of commission as well. So from now on we'll be able to live quite differently, just as we like. I feel so bright and happy, Kristine. It is lovely to have lots of money and not have to worry about anything. Isn't it?

MRS LINDE: Yes, well, at any rate, it must be lovely to have enough for the essentials.

NORA: No, no, not just enough for the essentials, but lots and lots and lots of money.

MRS LINDE: (*Smiling*) Nora, Nora, you still haven't learnt to be sensible, have you? Even when we were at school, you always liked spending money.

NORA: (*Laughing quietly*) Yes, that's what Torvald always says. (*She wags her finger.*) But Nora Nora isn't as silly as you think. And I certainly haven't had a chance to spend any money. We've both had to work.

MRS LINDE: You as well?

NORA: Yes, I did bits and pieces, you know, needlework and

crochet and embroidery and that sort of thing. (*Casually*)
And other work as well. I expect you know that Torvald left
the Civil Service when we got married. There was no
prospect of promotion in his department and he really
needed a higher salary. But the first year he overworked and
pushed himself far too hard. He had to take on all sorts of
extra work, so you can imagine, he was slaving away day and
night. He couldn't keep it up and in the end he became
dangerously ill. Then the doctors said he would have to go
and spend some time in the south.

MRS LINDE: Yes, you were in Italy a whole year, weren't you?

NORA: Yes, that's right. It wasn't easy to arrange, I can tell you.
Ivar had just been born. But obviously we had to go. Oh, it
was a wonderful trip, lovely. And it saved Torvald's life. But
it cost an awful lot of money, Kristine.

MRS LINDE: I'm sure it did.

NORA: Four thousand, eight hundred kroner. That's a lot, isn't
it?

MRS LINDE: Yes. You're lucky to have had it when you needed it.

NORA: I should explain, we got it from my father.

MRS LINDE: Ah. Wasn't it about that time that he died?

NORA: Yes, Kristine, just about then. And the awful thing was, I
wasn't able to go and nurse him. I was expecting Ivar any
day. And I had my poor sick Torvald to look after. Dear old
Father, he was so kind. I never saw him again, Kristine. It's
the worst thing that's happened since I got married.

MRS LINDE: I know how fond of him you were. So then you went
to Italy.

NORA: Yes. We had the money and the doctors told us not to
waste any time. So we left the next month.

MRS LINDE: And was your husband quite better when he came
back?

NORA: Fit as a fiddle.

MRS LINDE: But then . . . why the doctor?

NORA: What?

MRS LINDE: I thought I heard the maid say the gentleman who
arrived the same time as I did was a doctor.

NORA: Oh, yes, that was Dr Rank. But he's not here professionally. He's our closest friend and we always see him at least once a day. No, Torvald hasn't been ill at all since we got back. And the children are fit and healthy, and so am I. (*Jumps up and claps her hands.*) Oh, God, Kristine, it's so wonderful to be alive and happy! . . . I'm sorry, I am terrible, just going on and on about myself. (*Sits down next to* MRS LINDE *on a stool and puts her arms in her lap.*) You mustn't be angry with me. Tell me, is it true you didn't love your husband? Why did you marry him?

MRS LINDE: My mother was still alive then: she was bedridden and helpless. And then I had two younger brothers to look after. I didn't think it would be right to turn down his offer.

NORA: No, I can understand that. Was he quite rich then?

MRS LINDE: He was fairly well off, yes. But his business was rather precarious, Nora. And when he died, the whole thing collapsed and there was nothing left.

NORA: Then what?

MRS LINDE: Well, I just had to struggle through, first by opening a little shop, then a school, and then whatever else I could think of. These last three years have been like one long non-stop workday. Now it's over, Nora. My mother doesn't need me any more, she died. Nor do the boys. They've gone into business, they can look after themselves.

NORA: You must feel very relieved now . . .

MRS LINDE: No. Just hopelessly futile. No one to live for any more. (*Gets up nervously.*) That's why I couldn't stand it stuck away in that out-of-the-way hole. It must be easier to find something here to occupy my mind, something I can take an interest in. If I could only be lucky enough to find something permanent here, some kind of office job . . .

NORA: But that's terribly tiring, Kristine, and you look worn out already. It'd be much better for you to go and spend a few days at some spa.

MRS LINDE: (*Moving over to the window*) I don't have a father to pay all my expenses, Nora.

NORA: (*Rising*) Oh, don't be angry with me!

MRS LINDE: (*Walking towards her*) Don't you be angry with me,
Nora dear. The worst thing about the kind of situation I'm in
is that it fills you with bitterness. You have no one to work
for, and yet you have to put all your energy into it. You have
to live, and so you get selfish. When you were telling me
about your piece of good luck, I was more pleased for my
sake than for yours, if you can believe it.

NORA: Why? Oh, I see. You mean you thought perhaps Torvald
could do something for you?

MRS LINDE: I was thinking that, yes.

NORA: Well, I'm sure he will, Kristine. Leave it to me. I shall
work out some very, very subtle way to lead up to it and I
shall think of something charming to put him in a good
mood. I'd really love to help you.

MRS LINDE: It's very good of you, Nora, to take so much trouble.
Especially as you know so little about the trials and
tribulations of life.

NORA: I know so little . . .?

MRS LINDE: (*Smiling*) Well, except for a bit of needlework, of
course. You're a child, Nora.

NORA: (*Throwing her head back and crossing the room*) You
shouldn't be so patronizing.

MRS LINDE: Shouldn't I?

NORA: You're just like everyone else. Nobody thinks I'm capable
of doing anything really serious . . .

MRS LINDE: Now, now . . .

NORA: . . . or that I've ever had to face any real problems in this
hard world.

MRS LINDE: But, Nora dear, you've just told me about all your
difficulties.

NORA: Oh, that, that was nothing! (*Quietly*) I haven't told you
about the really important thing.

MRS LINDE: What really important thing? What do you mean?

NORA: You look down on me, Kristine. But you shouldn't. I
know you're very proud of having worked so hard and so
long to help your mother.

MRS LINDE: I'm sure I don't look down on anyone. But it is true

it makes me proud *and* happy to think I was able to make my
mother's last years relatively comfortable.

NORA: And you're proud of what you were able to do for your
brothers.

MRS LINDE: I think I have a right to be.

NORA: So do I. But I'll tell you something, Kristine. There is one
thing I can be proud and happy about as well.

MRS LINDE: I'm sure there is. What is it?

NORA: Keep your voice down. Torvald might hear us. He
mustn't ever find out about it. Nor must anyone, Kristine.
No one except you.

MRS LINDE: What? Find out about what?

NORA: Come here. (*Brings her over to the sofa and sits next to her.*)
You see . . . There's one thing I can be proud and happy
about. I saved Torvald's life.

MRS LINDE: Saved his life? How?

NORA: I told you about our trip to Italy. Torvald wouldn't have
recovered if he hadn't been able to go on it.

MRS LINDE: Yes, so your father gave you the money you needed.

NORA: (*Smiling*) Yes, that's what Torvald thinks, and so does
everyone else. But . . .

MRS LINDE: But what . . .?

NORA: Father didn't give us a penny. I got hold of the money
myself.

MRS LINDE: You did? All of it?

NORA: Four thousand, eight hundred kroner. What do you think
of that?

MRS LINDE: Yes, but how, Nora, how could you? Did you win it
in the lottery?

NORA: (*Scornfully*) In the lottery? (*Snorts.*) There wouldn't have
been anything very clever about that, would there?

MRS LINDE: Well then, where did you get it from?

NORA: (*Humming and smiling mysteriously*) Aha!

MRS LINDE: You couldn't possibly have borrowed it.

NORA: Oh, couldn't I? And why not?

MRS LINDE: Well, wives aren't allowed to borrow without their
husband's consent.

NORA: (*Tossing her head*) Oh, when a wife's got a bit of business sense and knows how to use her intelligence . . .

MRS LINDE: But, Nora, I don't understand at all . . .

NORA: You don't have to. Anyway, who said I'd borrowed it? There's more than one way to get hold of money. (*Flops back into the sofa.*) You never know, I might have got it from an admirer. When you're as attractive as I am . . .

MRS LINDE: Oh, don't be so silly.

NORA: You must be bursting with curiosity, Kristine.

MRS LINDE: Listen, Nora, are you sure you haven't done something rash?

NORA: (*Sitting up straight*) Is it rash to save your husband's life?

MRS LINDE: I think it's rash if you do it without his knowledge . . .

NORA: But that was the whole point, to do it without him finding out! God, don't you understand? We never intended him to find out how dangerously ill he was. The doctors came to see me and told me his life was in danger and that nothing could save him but a rest cure in the south. Do you think I didn't try to wheedle him into it first? I told him how lovely it would be for me to go abroad like all the other young brides, I cried and begged, I said he should think of my condition and that he ought to be considerate and humour me; finally, I suggested he might borrow the money. Well, that really made him angry, Kristine. He told me I was frivolous and said it was his duty as a husband not to give way to all my whims and impulses, I think he called them. All right, I thought, but you've still got to be saved – and I worked out a way to do it . . .

MRS LINDE: Didn't your husband find out from your father that the money hadn't come from him?

NORA: No, never. It was about that time my father died. I had thought of explaining it to him and asking him not to say anything. But he was terribly ill and sadly it was never necessary.

MRS LINDE: And you've never confessed to your husband since?

NORA: Good heavens, no, what a suggestion. He's got such strict views about that sort of thing. And besides, it would be a terrible blow to Torvald's masculine self-esteem, he'd find it so painful and humiliating to think he owed me something. It would completely unbalance our relationship. It would be the end of our beautiful, happy home.

MRS LINDE: Won't you ever tell him?

NORA: (*Pensively, half smiling*) Yes. Maybe one day I will. But not for years and years, not until I've stopped being so pretty. No, don't laugh. What I mean is not until Torvald's stopped being so fond of me, not until he's stopped enjoying it when I dance for him, or dress up and recite. Then it might be a good idea to have something up my sleeve . . . (*Breaking off*) Oh, I do talk rubbish, don't I? That could never happen. Well, what do you think of my great secret, Kristine? See, I am good for something after all, aren't I? But it's been a terrible worry, all this, you can imagine. It's not been at all easy to keep up with my payments. You see, in the world of business, there are things called instalments, and there's something else called quarterly interest. And they're always extremely difficult to get hold of. I've just had to save a little here and a little there, you know, whenever I could. I couldn't possibly put anything aside out of the housekeeping money, because Torvald had to be properly looked after. I couldn't let the children go around badly dressed, so I felt I had to spend everything I was given for them, dear little things.

MRS LINDE: Poor Nora. I suppose it all had to come out of your allowance, did it?

NORA: That's right. It was my responsibility, after all. Whenever Torvald used to give me money for new clothes or anything like that, I never used more than half of it. I always bought whatever was cheapest and simplest. Thank God things always suit me so well, Torvald never suspected anything. But it was often very difficult, Kristine. Because it's lovely to have beautiful clothes, isn't it?

MRS LINDE: Yes, it must be.

NORA: I found other ways of making money, as well. I was very lucky last winter, I managed to get a whole lot of copying work. I locked myself up every evening and sat up writing long into the night. I often used to feel really worn out. And yet in a way it was quite fun sitting up like that and working and earning money. It was almost like being a man.

MRS LINDE: And how much of it have you been able to pay off?

NORA: Well, I'm not quite sure, really. You see, it's rather complicated, keeping track of these financial dealings. All I know is that I've paid out everything I've managed to scrape together. There were times when I couldn't see any way out. (*Smiles*.) Then I used to sit here and think about a rich old man, who'd fallen madly in love with me . . .

MRS LINDE: What! Who?

NORA: Don't interrupt . . . and then he died, and when they opened his will, they found he'd written in big, bold letters: 'All my money is to be paid over to the adorable Mrs Nora Helmer. In cash.'

MRS LINDE: But who was he, Nora?

NORA: Oh, really, don't you understand? He was a fantasy, he didn't exist at all, I just sat here and imagined him when I couldn't think how I was going to get hold of the money. Anyway, it doesn't matter now. As far as I'm concerned, he can stay where he is, dreary old man. I couldn't care less about him or his will, my worries are over. (*Jumps up*.) Oh, God, Kristine, isn't it marvellous? No more worries! And if there's nothing to worry about any more, I can be free. I can have fun and play games with the children. I can spend some time on the house and make everything pretty and nice, the way Torvald likes it. And then it'll be spring soon and all those endless blue skies. And perhaps we'll be able to travel. I might see the sea again. It's really wonderful, isn't it, to be alive and happy!

(*The doorbell rings*.)

MRS LINDE: (*Rising*) There's someone at the front door. Perhaps I'd better go.

NORA: No, don't. I'm not expecting anyone. I expect it's someone for Torvald.

MAID: (*In the doorway*) Excuse me, madam, there's a gentleman here to see Mr Helmer. The doctor's still with him, so I wasn't sure . . .

NORA: Who is it?

KROGSTAD: (*In the doorway*) Good morning, Mrs Helmer.

(MRS LINDE *starts and turns to look out of the window.* NORA *anxiously takes a step towards him and speaks quickly.*)

NORA: What are you doing here? Why do you want to see my husband?

KROGSTAD: It's to do with the bank. I have a minor post in the Joint Stock Bank, and I understand your husband is to be our new manager.

NORA: So you're . . .

KROGSTAD: Simply here on dull routine business, Mrs Helmer. That's all.

NORA: Then would you be so good as to use the business entrance?

(*She nods indifferently to him and closes the door leading to the hall. Then she crosses to the stove and attends to the fire.*)

MRS LINDE: Nora, who was that?

NORA: A lawyer, a Mr Krogstad.

MRS LINDE: So it was him.

NORA: Do you know him?

MRS LINDE: I used to. Years ago. He used to work in a solicitor's office in our town.

NORA: That's right.

MRS LINDE: He's changed.

NORA: He had rather an unhappy marriage.

MRS LINDE: And he's a widower, isn't he?

NORA: With several children. That's better, I think it's caught now.

(*Closes the stove door and moves the rocking chair a little to one side.*)

MRS LINDE: Apparently he's dabbled in all sorts of different businesses.

NORA: Has he? Very likely. I wouldn't know. Anyway, don't let's talk about business, it's so boring.

(DR RANK *enters from Helmer's study.*)

RANK: (*In the doorway*) No, no, I'll be in your way. I'd rather go and have a chat with your wife. (*Closes the door and notices* MRS LINDE.) Oh, I'm sorry. I seem to be in the way here as well.

NORA: Not at all. (*Introduces them.*) Dr Rank. Mrs Linde.

RANK: Ah. That's a name I've often heard in this house. I think I passed you on the stairs when I arrived.

MRS LINDE: Yes. Stairs take me a long time. I find them rather an effort.

RANK: Have you had some sort of internal trouble?

MRS LINDE: No, it's just overwork, really.

RANK: Are you sure? So you've come up to town to go to all those restful parties, have you?

MRS LINDE: I've come to look for a job.

RANK: Of course, that's an infallible cure for overwork.

MRS LINDE: One has to live, Doctor.

RANK: Yes, that seems to be the general opinion.

NORA: Now, Dr Rank, you know very well you want to live as much as anyone else.

RANK: You're right. However miserable I am, I want the pain to drag on as long as possible. And all my patients are the same. So are the morally ill. At this very moment one of those moral invalids is in there talking to Helmer.

MRS LINDE: (*Softly*) Oh!

NORA: Who's that?

RANK: Oh, no one you know, his name is Krogstad, he's a lawyer, and he's rotten to the core. But even he began by saying, as if he were making some breathtaking revelation, that he had to live.

NORA: Why does he want to see Torvald?

RANK: No idea. I gathered it was something about the Joint Stock Bank.

NORA: I didn't know Krog . . . I mean, I didn't know this Mr Krogstad had anything to do with the bank.

RANK: Yes, he does have some sort of job there. (*To* MRS LINDE.) I don't know whether this sort of thing happens where you

come from, but there are people here who spend their time
panting around, trying to root out moral derelicts and then
employing them in some profitable position, just so that they
can keep an eye on them. And meanwhile honest, healthy
men are left out in the cold.

MRS LINDE: Well, I suppose it's the sick that most need looking
after.

RANK: (*Shrugging his shoulders*) That's just what I mean. That's
the sort of attitude that turns society into a hospital.
(NORA, *who has been buried in her own thoughts, half stifles a
sudden burst of laughter and claps her hands.*)
What are you laughing at? Have you any idea what society is?

NORA: I couldn't care less about your boring old society. I was
laughing about something else altogether . . . I just thought
of something extremely funny. Tell me, Dr Rank . . . is
everyone who works at the bank dependent on Torvald now?

RANK: I don't see what's so funny about that.

NORA: (*Smiling and humming*) Oh, never mind, never mind.
(*Wanders around the room.*) I find it terribly amusing to think
that we have, I mean, that Torvald has so much influence
over so many people's lives. (*Takes the bag out of her pocket.*)
Dr Rank, would you like a little macaroon?

RANK: Ah, macaroons, is it? I thought they were illegal in this
house.

NORA: Yes, but these were given to me by Kristine.

MRS LINDE: Me? I . . .

NORA: It's all right, nothing to worry about. You weren't to know
Torvald had outlawed them. The thing is, he's afraid they'll
rot my teeth. But it's not going to hurt just this once, is it,
Doctor? Here you are. (*Puts a macaroon into his mouth.*) One
for you, Kristine. And I'll have one too. Just a tiny one. Two
at the most. (*Wanders around again.*) I feel terribly happy.
There's only one thing in the world I really long to do.

RANK: What's that?

NORA: It's just something I really long to say in front of Torvald.

RANK: Go on then, what's stopping you?

NORA: I don't dare, it's so horrible.

MRS LINDE: Horrible?

RANK: Well, then, perhaps it wouldn't be very advisable. But you can tell us what it is you really long to say in front of Helmer.

NORA: I really long to say: hell and damnation.

RANK: You're mad.

MRS LINDE: Good heavens, Nora . . .

RANK: Say it. Here he comes.

NORA: (*Hiding the bag of macaroons*) Sh, sh, sh!

(HELMER *enters from his study with his hat in his hand and his overcoat over his arm.*)

(*Going over to him*) Did you get rid of him, Torvald?

HELMER: Yes, he's gone.

NORA: Let me introduce you. This is Kristine, she's just arrived in town.

HELMER: Kristine? I'm sorry, I don't think I . . .

NORA: Mrs Linde, dear. Mrs Kristine Linde.

HELMER: Oh, yes. Erm, you must be a schoolfriend of my wife . . .

MRS LINDE: Yes, we knew each other a long time ago.

NORA: And she's come all this way to talk to you.

HELMER: To me? I don't understand.

MRS LINDE: Well, that's not really . . .

NORA: Kristine's terribly clever at office work, and what she really longs to do is to work for somebody very experienced, so that she can learn even more about it.

HELMER: Sounds very sensible, Mrs Linde.

NORA: And when she heard that you'd been made bank manager, someone sent her a telegram about it, she travelled up here as soon as she could and . . . Don't you think you could do something for Kristine? For my sake, Torvald? Mm?

HELMER: It's not impossible. I assume you're a widow, Mrs Linde?

MRS LINDE: Yes.

HELMER: And you've had some business experience?

MRS LINDE: Quite a lot, yes.

HELMER: Then it's very likely I'll be able to find you a place.

NORA: (*Clapping her hands*) There you are, you see!

HELMER: You timed your arrival very well, Mrs Linde . . .

MRS LINDE: Oh, how can I ever thank you . . . ?

HELMER: Think nothing of it. (*Puts on his overcoat.*) Well, you
must excuse me now . . .

RANK: Just a minute, I'll come with you.
(*He fetches his fur coat from the hall and warms it in front of the
fire.*)

NORA: Don't be long, dear.

HELMER: I shan't be more than an hour.

NORA: Are you leaving as well, Kristine?

MRS LINDE: (*Putting on her overcoat*) Yes, I must go and look for a
room.

HELMER: Perhaps you'd like to walk down with us?

NORA: (*Helping her*) It's a bind we're so short of room. I don't
know if we could manage . . .

MRS LINDE: Oh, no, I wouldn't dream of it. Goodbye, Nora dear,
and thank you for everything.

NORA: Goodbye for now. Of course you must come back for
dinner this evening. And you too, Dr Rank. What's that?

RANK: I said, if I'm well enough.

NORA: If you're well enough? I'm sure you'll be well enough. As
long as you wrap up warm.
(*Further exchanges as they go out into the hall. The children's
voices are heard outside on the stairs.*)
Here they are! Here they are!
(*She runs to open the front door.* ANNE-MARIE, *the nurse, comes
in with the children.*)
Come in, come in! (*She bends down to kiss them.*) Sweet.
Aren't you? You see, Kristine? Aren't they lovely?

RANK: Don't let's just stand around chattering in the draught.

HELMER: Come along, Mrs Linde. This is where it becomes
unbearable for anyone who isn't a mother.
(DR RANK, HELMER *and* MRS LINDE *go down the stairs.*
ANNE-MARIE *enters the room with the children.* NORA *follows,
closing the door behind her.*)

NORA: You're looking very cheeky, where did you get those
healthy little red faces? You look like apples and roses.

(*The children are all talking at once during what follows.*)
Have you had a nice time? Good. You gave Emmy and Bob a
ride on your sledge, did you? Both at once? Aren't you a
clever little boy, Ivar? Give her to me a minute, Anne-Marie.
She's like a little doll, aren't you, sweetie? Mm?
(*She takes the smallest from* ANNE-MARIE *and dances round
with her.*)
All right, all right, Mummy will dance with Bob as well.
What? Snowballs? Oh, I wish I'd been with you. No, just a
minute, Anne-Marie, I'll take their things off. No, let me,
please, it's such fun. You look terribly cold, why don't you
go in for a bit? There's some hot coffee on the stove in there.
(ANNE-MARIE *exits left.* NORA *takes the children's things off,
throwing them down all over the place, letting the children chatter
away all at once.*)
A big what ran after you? A dog? He didn't bite you, did he?
Dogs never bite lovely little dolls. Ivar! Stop it, you mustn't
look at the parcels. Aha, wouldn't you like to know? No, it's
something absolutely horrible. Now. Shall we play a game?
Let's play a game. Hide-and-seek? Bob, you hide first. Me?
All right, I'll hide first.
(*She and the children play hide-and-seek in the living room and
the room adjoining it on the right. Finally,* NORA *hides under the
table, the children come storming in, look for her but can't find
her, hear her smothered laughter, rush over to the table, lift the
cloth and see her. Great excitement. She creeps out from under the
table, as if to frighten them. More excitement. Meanwhile, there
has been a knock at the front door which no one has noticed. The
door is half opened and* KROGSTAD *appears. He waits a
moment. The game continues.*)

KROGSTAD: Excuse me, Mrs Helmer . . .
NORA: (*Smothering a cry, turning round and half jumping*) Oh!
   What do you want?
KROGSTAD: I'm sorry to – er . . . the front door was open,
   someone must have forgotten to close it . . .
NORA: (*Getting up*) My husband is out, Mr Krogstad.
KROGSTAD: I know.

NORA: Then . . . what is it you want?

KROGSTAD: A word with you.

NORA: With me? (*Quietly to the children*) Go in and see Anne-Marie. No, there's nothing to worry about, he won't hurt me. And when he's gone, we'll play another game.
(*She takes the children over to the room on the left and closes the door behind them.*
(*Tense, uneasy*) You want to talk to me?

KROGSTAD: Yes.

NORA: Why today? It's not the first of the month yet.

KROGSTAD: No, I know, it's Christmas Eve. And if you want it to be a happy Christmas, it's up to you.

NORA: What do you want? I can't possibly get hold of it today.

KROGSTAD: There's no need to worry about that just at the moment. It's something else. Have you got a minute?

NORA: Yes. Yes, of course. Except . . .

KROGSTAD: Good. I was sitting in Olsen's restaurant just now, and I saw your husband passing down the street . . .

NORA: Well?

KROGSTAD: . . . with a lady.

NORA: What of it?

KROGSTAD: Might I be so bold as to ask whether that lady was a certain Mrs Linde?

NORA: Yes, it was.

KROGSTAD: Has she just arrived in town?

NORA: Yes, today.

KROGSTAD: Is she a close friend of yours?

NORA: Yes, she is. But I don't see . . .

KROGSTAD: I used to know her as well.

NORA: Yes.

KROGSTAD: Ah, she told you about all that, did she? I thought as much. Now, will you please give me a straight answer to this? Has Mrs Linde been given a job at the bank?

NORA: I don't know how you can have the face to interrogate me like this, Mr Krogstad. You are one of my husband's employees, after all. However, since you ask, I might as well tell you. Mrs Linde has been given a job there. On my recommendation, Mr Krogstad. Now you know.

KROGSTAD: So I guessed right.

NORA: (*Pacing round the room*) I think I do have a little bit of influence, you know. Just because I'm a woman, it doesn't mean I don't . . . So you see, Mr Krogstad, when one finds oneself in a subordinate position, one really needs to be careful not to offend anyone with . . . erm . . .

KROGSTAD: Influence.

NORA: Exactly.

KROGSTAD: (*A change of tone*) Mrs Helmer, I wonder if you'd be kind enough to use your influence on my behalf?

NORA: What? What do you mean?

KROGSTAD: Would you be so kind as to make sure I keep my subordinate position at the bank?

NORA: I don't understand. Why should anyone take it away from you?

KROGSTAD: Oh, there's no point pretending you don't know anything about it. I realize it can't be very pleasant for your friend to be pushed together with me. And now I realize who's responsible for hounding me out.

NORA: I assure you I . . .

KROGSTAD: Yes, yes, well, never mind that. There's still time to stop it and I advise you to use your influence to do something about it.

NORA: But, Mr Krogstad, I've got no influence, really.

KROGSTAD: You just said . . .

NORA: I know, I know, but that was different. You can't really think I have that much influence over my husband.

KROGSTAD: Oh, I know your husband, we were students together. I know he's a bank manager, but I don't think you'll find him any more resolute than any other husband.

NORA: If you're going to insult my husband, I shall have to ask you to leave.

KROGSTAD: A lady of spirit.

NORA: I'm not afraid of you any more. By the New Year, all this will be behind me.

KROGSTAD: (*Controlling himself*) Now listen to me, Mrs Helmer.

If necessary, I'm prepared to fight for my little job at the bank as if I were fighting for my life.

NORA: Apparently.

KROGSTAD: It's not just the salary, you know. That's the last thing I'm worried about. It's something else . . . I'll tell you about it, shall I, explain it to you. I suppose you know, like everyone else, that a few years ago I . . . made a mistake.

NORA: I did hear something about it.

KROGSTAD: I was never brought to trial for it. But from then on, for me, all roads were blocked. You know what business I went into then. I had to do something; and I don't think I've been as bad as many of them. But now I've got to put all that behind me. My sons are growing up, I've got to win back as much public respectability as I can, for their sake. For me that job at the bank was the first step on the ladder. And now your husband wants to kick me off again, back into the mud.

NORA: But for God's sake, Mr Krogstad, it really isn't in my power to help you.

KROGSTAD: You only say that, because you don't want to help me. But I have the means to force you.

NORA: You aren't going to tell my husband I owe you money?

KROGSTAD: Well? Suppose I do?

NORA: That would be a wicked thing to do. (*Tearfully*) That secret is my pride and my happiness, if he were to find out about it in such a crude, ugly way, from you . . . It would put me in the most frightfully unpleasant position.

KROGSTAD: Unpleasant, is that all?

NORA: (*Vehemently*) All right then, do it. It'll be the worse for you. Then my husband really will see how vicious you are and you're bound to lose your job.

KROGSTAD: I asked you if it was just a bit of domestic unpleasantness you were afraid of?

NORA: If my husband does find out about it, he will of course pay whatever's outstanding at once and then we need have nothing more to do with you.

KROGSTAD: (*Moving a step nearer*) Listen, Mrs Helmer. Either you have a very poor memory, or else you haven't much of a clue about business. I can see I'm going to have to give you a course of basic instruction.

NORA: What do you mean?

KROGSTAD: When your husband was ill, you came to me to borrow four thousand, eight hundred kroner.

NORA: You were the only one I knew of.

KROGSTAD: I promised to raise the money for you . . .

NORA: And you did.

KROGSTAD: I promised to raise the money for you on certain conditions. But at the time, you were so preoccupied with your husband's illness and so anxious to get hold of enough for the journey, I don't think you paid very much attention to the technicalities of the contract. That's why I feel it would be not inappropriate to remind you of them. Now. I promised to raise the money for you in return for an IOU, which I drew up.

NORA: Yes, and which I signed.

KROGSTAD: Right. But then I added another clause at the bottom, which said your father would act as guarantor for the loan, and which needed your father's signature.

NORA: He did sign it.

KROGSTAD: The date was left blank, so that your father could fill it in himself when he signed the contract. Do you remember?

NORA: I think so, yes . . .

KROGSTAD: I gave you the contract to post to your father, didn't I?

NORA: Yes.

KROGSTAD: You must have sent it off to him straight away. Because five or six days later you brought it in to me with your father's signature. Whereupon I handed over the money.

NORA: Well? I've kept my payments regular, haven't I?

KROGSTAD: More or less. But anyway, to go back to what we were discussing, I imagine that must have been a very difficult time for you, Mrs Helmer.

NORA: Yes, it was.

KROGSTAD: I believe your father was very ill as well.

NORA: He was dying.

KROGSTAD: And did die shortly afterwards?

NORA: Yes.

KROGSTAD: Tell me, Mrs Helmer, do you by any chance remember what day your father died? The date, I mean.

NORA: Father died on the twenty-ninth of September.

KROGSTAD: That's right. I made inquiries. And this is where we come to the unusual feature of the case . . . (*He produces a document.*) . . . which I must say I'm at a loss to explain.

NORA: Unusual feature? I don't think . . .

KROGSTAD: The unusual feature of the case, Mrs Helmer, is that your father signed this contract three days after he died.

NORA: What? I don't understand . . .

KROGSTAD: Your father died on September the twenty-ninth. Now, look at this. Here your father has dated his signature October the second. Now, that is rather unusual, Mrs Helmer, wouldn't you agree?

(NORA *is silent.*)

Not easy to explain, is it?

(NORA *still doesn't answer.*)

It also struck me that the words October the second and the year were not in your father's handwriting, but in a handwriting I think I recognize. Well, I'm sure there's an explanation for that, your father might have forgotten to date his signature and someone else has added a date at random, not knowing about his death. There's nothing wrong with that. What is vitally important is the signature itself. I suppose it is genuine, Mrs Helmer? Your father really did sign here, did he?

NORA: (*After a short silence, throwing her head back and confronting him defiantly*) No, he didn't. I did.

KROGSTAD: Mrs Helmer . . . you realize that's a very dangerous confession?

NORA: Why? You'll have your money soon enough.

KROGSTAD: May I ask you a question? Why didn't you send your father the contract?

NORA: I couldn't. Father was very ill. If I'd asked him for his signature, I'd have had to have told him why I needed the money. He was so ill, I couldn't have told him my husband's life was in danger. It was impossible.

KROGSTAD: Then you would have done better to cancel your trip.

NORA: I couldn't possibly. It saved my husband's life. I couldn't possibly cancel it.

KROGSTAD: But you were cheating me, or did that never occur to you?

NORA: I couldn't afford to worry about things like that. I didn't care about you. I hated you for making all those ruthless conditions, when you knew how dangerously ill my husband was.

KROGSTAD: Mrs Helmer, you obviously have no clear idea what you're guilty of. I can assure you that what I did was no more and no worse than that, and it totally destroyed my position in society.

NORA: What you did? Are you trying to tell me you took any risks to save your wife's life?

KROGSTAD: The law is not interested in motives.

NORA: Then the law is useless.

KROGSTAD: Useless or not, if I were to submit this contract to a court, you would be condemned by the law.

NORA: I don't believe it. You mean a daughter isn't allowed to spare her old, dying father worry and anxiety? A wife isn't allowed to save her husband's life? I don't know much about the law, but I'm sure there must be provisions made somewhere for that kind of situation. And if you don't know that, then all I can say is that you must be a pretty useless lawyer, Mr Krogstad.

KROGSTAD: That's as may be. But when it comes to business, the kind of business we're involved in, you can take my word for it I know what I'm talking about. All right. Now do what you like. But I'm telling you one thing: if I'm thrown out again, you're coming with me.

(*He bows and exits into the hall.* NORA *stands for a moment, thinking, then tosses her head back.*)

NORA: Hm! He's just trying to frighten me. I'm not as stupid
as that. (*Starts folding up the children's clothes, then pauses.*)
But . . .? No, no, it's impossible.

CHILDREN: (*In the left-hand doorway*) Mummy, the stranger's
gone now, Mummy.

NORA: Yes, I know. But you're not to tell anyone there was a
stranger here. Do you understand? Not even Daddy.

CHILDREN: Yes, Mummy. Are we going to play a game now?

NORA: No. No, not now.

CHILDREN: Oh, Mummy, you promised.

NORA: Yes, but I can't now. I've got so much to do. Come along
now, in you go, dears, in you go.

(*She pushes them gently into their room and closes the door behind
them. Then she sits on the sofa, embroiders a few stitches, then
gives up.*)

No. (*Puts down the embroidery, gets up, goes over to the hall
door and calls out.*) Helene! Bring the tree in. (*She crosses left
to the table, opens a drawer, pauses.*) No, it's impossible.

MAID: (*With the Christmas tree*) Where shall I put it, madam?

NORA: There. In the middle. I'll just move the table.

MAID: Is there anything else to be brought in?

NORA: No, thank you. I have everything I need.

(*The* MAID *puts down the tree and exits.*)

(*Decorating the tree*) A candle here . . . and flowers here . . .
Horrible man. Anyway, it's all a lot of nonsense. Not worth
worrying about. The Christmas tree's going to be lovely. I'll
do anything you want me to, Torvald, sing for you, dance for
you . . .

(HELMER *enters, with a bundle of papers under his arm.*)

Oh . . . back already?

HELMER: Yes. Has anyone been here?

NORA: Here? No.

HELMER: That's funny. I saw Krogstad leaving the house.

NORA: Really? Yes, that's right, Krogstad was here for a minute.

HELMER: Nora, he was here begging you to put in a good word
for him, wasn't he? I can tell just by looking at you.

NORA: Yes.

HELMER: And you were going to pretend it was your idea, weren't you? You weren't going to tell me he'd been here. Was that his suggestion, as well?

NORA: Yes, Torvald, but . . .

HELMER: Nora, really, how could you agree to something like that? How could you talk to that sort of man, let alone make promises to him? And then lie to me on top of everything.

NORA: Lie to you . . .?

HELMER: You said no one had been here. Didn't you? (*Wags his finger at her.*) My little songbird must never do that again. A songbird must have a clean beak, mustn't she, she mustn't sing out of tune. (*Puts his arm round her.*) Isn't that right? Yes, I thought so. (*Lets her go.*) Now, we'll say no more about it. (*Sits down by the stove.*) Isn't it warm and cosy here? (*He starts looking through his papers.* NORA *is busy with the Christmas tree. Short silence.*)

NORA: Torvald.

HELMER: Yes.

NORA: I'm really looking forward to the Stenborgs' fancy-dress ball the day after tomorrow.

HELMER: And I'm dying to see what you're going to surprise me with this time.

NORA: Oh, it's so silly!

HELMER: What?

NORA: I can't think of anything good. Everything seems so stupid and pointless.

HELMER: So you've found that out, have you, Nora?

NORA: (*Behind him, looking over the back of his chair*) Are you very busy, Torvald?

HELMER: Well . . .

NORA: What are those papers?

HELMER: They're to do with the bank.

NORA: Already?

HELMER: I've persuaded the outgoing manager to give me the authority to make the necessary staff and administration changes. I must get that done during Christmas week. I want all that sorted out by the New Year.

NORA: And that's why poor Krogstad . . .

HELMER: Mm.

NORA: (*Still leaning over the back of his chair and slowly ruffling his hair*) If you hadn't been so busy, Torvald, I would have asked you an enormous favour.

HELMER: And what might that be? Tell me.

NORA: Your taste is better than anyone's. And I really want to look nice at the fancy-dress ball. Couldn't you take charge of me, Torvald, and decide what I should be and what sort of costume I should wear?

HELMER: What, a stubborn little girl like you appealing for a saviour?

NORA: Yes, Torvald, I'll never be able to manage without your help.

HELMER: All right, I'll think about it, see what we come up with.

NORA: You're very kind to me. (*Moves over to the Christmas tree. Pause.*) Aren't those red flowers pretty? . . . Tell me, was it really so terrible, whatever it was Krogstad did wrong?

HELMER: Forgery. Have you any idea how serious that is?

NORA: But isn't it possible he was forced into it by necessity?

HELMER: Yes. Or else he just did it without thinking, like so many people. I'm not so heartless as to condemn a man irrevocably because of one isolated incident.

NORA: No, I know you're not, Torvald.

HELMER: A man can always regain his moral stature, if he openly confesses his crime and takes his punishment.

NORA: Punishment . . . ?

HELMER: But that wasn't Krogstad's method. He got out of it by trickery and deceit. And that's what makes him a moral cripple.

NORA: Don't you think . . . ?

HELMER: Think of the way a man with a guilty conscience has to live: lies, hypocrisy, pretence, even those nearest to him, even his wife and children can never see behind his mask. And the most dreadful thing about it is what happens to the children.

NORA: Why?

HELMER: Because an atmosphere of lies can infect and contaminate the whole life of a home. Every breath the children take in a house like that is full of disgusting germs.

NORA: (*Moving closer behind him*) Are you sure about that?

HELMER: My dear, as a lawyer, I've had more than enough experience of that sort of thing. Nearly all young criminals have had dishonest mothers.

NORA: Why do you say mothers?

HELMER: Because it usually is the mother's responsibility. Although, of course, the father can have the same effect. Any lawyer knows that. And yet Krogstad has been at home all these years, poisoning his own children with lies and deceit. That's why I say he's morally degenerate. (*Holds out his arms to her.*) And that's why my dear little Nora is going to promise me never to mention him again. Shake hands on it. Now, what's the matter? Give me your hand. Right. That's settled. Anyway, it would have been quite impossible for me to work with him, I can tell you. People like that literally make me feel physically ill.

NORA: (*Withdrawing her hand and moving over to the other side of the Christmas tree*) It's very warm in here. I've got so much to do.

HELMER: (*Standing and gathering up his papers*) Yes, and I ought to read through some of these papers before lunch. And I'll have a think about your costume as well. And I might even find a little something to wrap up in gold paper and hang on the Christmas tree. (*Puts his hand on her head.*) Darling little songbird.

(*He goes into the study and closes the door behind him.*)

NORA: (*Quietly, after a pause*) No. It's not true. It's impossible. Must be impossible.

ANNE-MARIE: (*In the doorway, left*) The children want to know if they can come in and see Mummy.

NORA: No. No, they mustn't, don't let them in. Keep them with you, Anne-Marie.

ANNE-MARIE: Very good, madam.

(*She closes the door.*)

NORA: (*Pale with terror*) Corrupt my children. Poison my home. (*Pause. She throws back her head.*) It's not true. It could never be true.

ACT TWO

The same room. In the corner, by the piano, is the Christmas tree, stripped, bedraggled, the candles burnt out. Nora's overcoat is on the sofa.

   NORA, *alone in the room, is pacing up and down restlessly. Finally she stops by the sofa and picks up her coat.*

NORA: (*Putting on her coat*) Who's that? (*Moves over to the door and listens.*) No, it's nobody. Of course not. Nobody would come on Christmas Day. Or tomorrow. Unless . . . (*Opens the door and looks out.*) No. Nothing in the letterbox. Nothing at all. (*Crosses the room.*) Oh, don't be silly. He didn't mean it. Of course he didn't, he couldn't do a thing like that. It's impossible. I have three children.

   (ANNE-MARIE *enters from the left, carrying a large cardboard box.*)

ANNE-MARIE: I finally found the box with the fancy-dress costumes.

NORA: Thank you. Put it down on the table.

ANNE-MARIE: (*Doing so*) But they're in an awful muddle.

NORA: I wish I could rip them up into a hundred thousand pieces.

ANNE-MARIE: Oh, there's no need to do that, they can easily be sorted out. All it needs is a bit of patience.

NORA: I'm going to get Mrs Linde over to help me.

ANNE-MARIE: Going out again? In this weather? You'll catch cold, madam, you will.

NORA: That wouldn't be the end of the world. How are the children?

ANNE-MARIE: Poor little things, they're playing with their Christmas presents, but . . .

NORA: Do they ask for me much?

ANNE-MARIE: They're so used to being with their Mummy.

NORA: Yes, well, Anne-Marie, from now on I'm not going to be able to spend so much time with them.

128

ANNE-MARIE: Little children can get used to anything.

NORA: Do you think so? Do you think they'd forget their mother if she went away for ever?

ANNE-MARIE: Went away for ever? What do you mean?

NORA: Listen, Anne-Marie, tell me. I've often thought about this, how could you bear to give your child away to strangers?

ANNE-MARIE: But I had to, I was going to be little Nora's nanny.

NORA: Yes, but surely you didn't want to?

ANNE-MARIE: Where else could I have found such a good place? A poor girl who's got herself into trouble has to make the best of things. That good-for-nothing man wasn't going to do anything for me.

NORA: But your daughter must have forgotten you.

ANNE-MARIE: No, she hasn't. She wrote to me when she was confirmed and again when she got married.

NORA: (*Putting her arms round her*) Dear old Anne-Marie, you were a good mother to me when I was little.

ANNE-MARIE: Poor little Nora, I was the only mother you had.

NORA: And if my children had no one, I know you'd . . . anyway, that's all a lot of nonsense. (*Opens the box.*) Go back and look after them. I'm going to . . . Tomorrow you'll see how lovely I shall be.

ANNE-MARIE: Yes, I'm sure there'll be no one at the ball as lovely as Nora.

(*She exits, left.*)

NORA: (*Beginning to unpack the box, but very soon losing interest*) I don't dare go out. Suppose someone came. Suppose something happened here at home. Don't be so stupid. No one's going to come. Just don't think about it. Must brush my muff. Lovely gloves, aren't they lovely? Stop it. Stop it! One, two, three, four, five, six . . . (*Cries out.*) Oh, he's here! (*She moves towards the door, then hesitates.* MRS LINDE *enters from the hall, where she has taken off her overcoat.*) Oh, it's you, Kristine. There's no one else out there, is there? It's very good of you to come.

MRS LINDE: I hear you called in to see me.

NORA: Yes, I was just passing. There's something I wanted you to give me a hand with. Let's sit over here on the sofa. Now. Tomorrow evening there's a fancy-dress ball at Consul Stenborg's, upstairs, and Torvald wants me to go as a Neapolitan fishergirl and dance the tarantella, which I learned when we were in Capri.

MRS LINDE: I see, you'll give them the full performance, will you?

NORA: Well, that's what Torvald wants me to do. This is the costume, look. Torvald had it made for me in Italy. But it's got so badly ripped, I don't know . . .

MRS LINDE: Oh, we'll soon fix that. It's just the trimming's come a bit loose in one or two places, that's all. Needle and thread, have you got? That's it, that's everything we need.

NORA: It's very good of you, this.

MRS LINDE: (*Sewing*) So you're going in disguise tomorrow, are you, Nora? Do you know, I think I'll come round for a minute, so I can see you in all your finery. Oh, I forgot to thank you for a very pleasant evening yesterday.

NORA: (*Crossing the room*) Oh, I didn't think it was as pleasant as it usually is, yesterday. You should have arrived in town a bit sooner, Kristine. Torvald really understands how to make a home lovely and welcoming.

MRS LINDE: I think you do as well. You're not your father's daughter for nothing. Is Dr Rank always as lugubrious as he was yesterday evening?

NORA: No, last night it was much more noticeable than usual. The thing is, you see, he's very seriously ill, poor man. He's got spinal consumption. Apparently his father was a disgusting creature, who kept a string of mistresses and all that sort of thing. And, you see, that's why his health has been so poor ever since he was a child.

MRS LINDE: (*Putting down her sewing*) My dear Nora, wherever do you find out about things like that?

NORA: (*Walking up and down*) Oh well, if you have three children, you have these . . . women visiting you from time to time who are sort of half-doctors and know about these things. And they talk about this and that, you know.

MRS LINDE: (*Starts sewing again, after a short silence*) Does Dr
  Rank come here every day?

NORA: Every single day. Torvald's known him since they were
  boys, he's his best friend, and he's a very good friend of mine
  as well. He sort of belongs.

MRS LINDE: But tell me, do you think he's a sincere man? I mean,
  doesn't he have a tendency to be a bit of a flatterer?

NORA: No, quite the contrary. Whatever makes you think that?

MRS LINDE: When you introduced me to him yesterday, he said
  he'd often heard my name in this house. And yet later on I
  noticed your husband didn't have the slightest idea who I
  was. So how could Dr Rank . . . ?

NORA: But that's true, Kristine. Torvald's incredibly possessive,
  he's always saying he wants to keep me all to himself. When
  we were first married, he used to get quite jealous if I
  mentioned any of my friends from home. So of course I
  stopped doing that. But I often talk to Dr Rank about that
  sort of thing, you know, he seems to like it.

MRS LINDE: Listen, Nora. You're still a child in all sorts of ways.
  I'm a lot older than you and I'm a bit more experienced. I
  want to say something to you: you should stop all this with
  Dr Rank.

NORA: All what?

MRS LINDE: I mean, the whole thing. Yesterday you were talking
  about a rich admirer, who was going to get hold of some
  money for you . . .

NORA: Yes, someone who doesn't exist, worse luck. What about
  it?

MRS LINDE: Is Dr Rank well off?

NORA: Yes, he is.

MRS LINDE: And he has no dependants?

NORA: No, why?

MRS LINDE: And he comes here every day?

NORA: Yes, I told you.

MRS LINDE: He seems to have more stamina than tact.

NORA: I don't know what you're talking about.

MRS LINDE: Don't pretend with me, Nora. Do you think I can't

guess who lent you that four thousand, eight hundred
kroner?

NORA: You must be out of your mind. Is that really what you
think? A friend of ours, who comes here every day? The
situation would be absolutely intolerable.

MRS LINDE: So it really isn't him?

NORA: No, I promise you. I'd never have dreamt of it for a
moment. In any case, at that time he didn't have any money
to lend. He's inherited it all since.

MRS LINDE: Well, I think that was probably lucky for you,
Nora.

NORA: No, I'd never have dreamt of asking Dr Rank . . . Mind
you, I'm quite sure if I had asked him . . .

MRS LINDE: Which of course you never would.

NORA: Of course. And I can't think that the situation would ever
arise. But I'm quite sure that if I did speak to Dr Rank . . .

MRS LINDE: Behind your husband's back?

NORA: The other business was behind his back. I must get out of
that, I must.

MRS LINDE: Yes, that's what I was saying yesterday. But . . .

NORA: (*Pacing up and down*) A man can deal with these things so
much better than a woman . . .

MRS LINDE: Yes, if he's your husband.

NORA: Anyway, it's all a lot of nonsense. (*Stands still.*) When
you've paid all the money, you get the IOU back, don't you?

MRS LINDE: Obviously.

NORA: And you can tear it up into a hundred thousand pieces and
burn it, filthy, disgusting bit of paper.

MRS LINDE: (*Looks at her severely, puts her sewing down and gets up
deliberately*) Nora, you're hiding something from me.

NORA: Does it show?

MRS LINDE: What is it, Nora? Something's happened since
yesterday morning, hasn't it?

NORA: (*Moving towards her*) Kristine! (*Stops, listening.*) Ssh, that's
Torvald. Listen, go in there with the children for a bit.
Torvald can't bear seeing people dressmaking. Get Anne-
Marie to give you a hand.

MRS LINDE: (*Collecting her things together*) All right. But I'm not leaving the house until we've had a serious talk.

(*She exits left, as* HELMER *enters from the hall.*)

NORA: (*Moving towards him*) I've missed you terribly, Torvald.

HELMER: Was that that dressmaker girl . . .?

NORA: No, it's Kristine. She's helping me to get my costume ready. It's going to look very nice, you know.

HELMER: Wasn't it an inspired idea of mine?

NORA: Marvellous! But don't you think it was good of me as well, to give in to you?

HELMER: (*Taking her chin in his hand*) Good of you? To give in to your husband? Get on with you, you little minx, I know you didn't mean it. Anyway, I shan't disturb you, I expect you want to try it on.

NORA: And you're going to do some work, are you?

HELMER: Yes. (*Shows her a pile of papers.*) I've just been down to the bank.

(*He moves towards the study.*)

NORA: Torvald.

HELMER: (*Stopping*) Yes.

NORA: Suppose your little squirrel were to ask you ever so nicely for a great big enormous favour . . .?

HELMER: Go on.

NORA: Would you say yes?

HELMER: Depends what it was.

NORA: Your squirrel would jump up and down and do all sorts of tricks for you, if you were nice and gave in . . .

HELMER: Come on, then, out with it.

NORA: Your lark would chirp and sing all over the place . . .

HELMER: But larks always do that anyway.

NORA: I'll be a little pixie and dance in the moonlight for you, Torvald.

HELMER: Nora, is it anything to do with what we were talking about this morning?

NORA: (*Going up to him*) Yes, Torvald, please, please . . .

HELMER: Have you really got the nerve to bring all that up again?

NORA: You must say yes, you must let Krogstad stay on at the bank.

HELMER: My dear Nora, I've already given his place to Mrs Linde.

NORA: Yes, that was terribly kind of you. But can't you just get rid of someone else instead of Krogstad?

HELMER: You really are incredibly stubborn. Just because you make some rash promise to put in a word for him, you expect me to . . .!

NORA: It's nothing to do with that, Torvald. It's for your sake. That man writes for the most despicable newspapers, you've told me that yourself. He could do you untold harm. I'm so terribly frightened of him . . .

HELMER: Oh, I see. It's old memories that are upsetting you, is it?

NORA: What do you mean?

HELMER: You're thinking of your father, I suppose.

NORA: Yes, that's right. Just remember the cruel slanders those malicious people used to write about Daddy in the papers. If the Ministry hadn't sent you over to investigate, and if you hadn't been so kind and helpful to him, I think he would have been dismissed.

HELMER: My dear Nora, there's a considerable difference between your father and me. As a civil servant, your father was by no means irreproachable. I am. And as long as I maintain my position, I hope I always will be.

NORA: No one knows what really unscrupulous people are capable of devising. We could be so well off now, in our peaceful little home, so quiet and happy and carefree . . . just you and I and the children. That's why I'm asking, Torvald, that's why it's so important to me . . .

HELMER: The more you plead for him, the more impossible it becomes for me to keep him on. People at the bank already know I've dismissed Krogstad. Suppose rumours got round that the new manager had let his mind be changed for him by his wife . . .

NORA: Well, what if they did . . .?

HELMER: Oh, well, of course, that's nothing, as long as a certain stubborn little lady could have her way. I'd only become the laughing stock of the entire staff and make people think I was totally dependent on outside influences. Believe me, I'd soon suffer the consequences. Anyway . . . there's one thing that makes it quite impossible for Krogstad to stay on at the bank, as long as I'm manager.

NORA: What's that?

HELMER: If necessary I might be able to overlook his moral limitations . . .

NORA: Yes, I'm sure you could, Torvald.

HELMER: And I gather he's quite efficient. But the thing is, he was a friend of mine at school. It was one of those injudicious friendships one so often has cause to regret in later life. Anyway, I might as well tell you what it is right away: he actually calls me by my Christian name. It's so tactless of him, and he always does it, even when other people are there. In fact, he seems to think he's entitled to be as familiar as he likes, he never misses a chance to come out with it, Torvald this, Torvald that. I don't mind telling you, I find it intensely embarrassing. He would make my whole position at the bank quite intolerable.

NORA: Torvald, you can't honestly mean that.

HELMER: Can't I? Why not?

NORA: Well, it's so . . . petty.

HELMER: What do you mean? Petty? Do you think I'm petty?

NORA: No, of course not, Torvald. It's just . . .

HELMER: Well, if you say my behaviour is petty, that must mean I am as well. Petty! I see. Well, we shall have to make sure we put a stop to that, shan't we? (*Walks over to the door and calls out.*) Helene!

NORA: What are you doing?

HELMER: (*Looking through his papers*) Making a decision. (*The* MAID *enters.*)
Now. Take this letter. Go down and find a messenger right away and tell him to deliver it. Quickly. The address is on the envelope. Here's some money.
(*She exits with the letter.*)
(*Arranging his papers*) So much for you, little Miss Obstinate.

NORA: (*Breathlessly*) Torvald . . . what was in the letter?

HELMER: Krogstad's dismissal.

NORA: Get it back, Torvald. There's still time. Oh, Torvald, please get it back. For my sake . . . and for yours. For the children's sake. Please, Torvald, listen. You don't know what this could do to us.

HELMER: Too late.

NORA: Yes, it is too late.

HELMER: My dear Nora, I forgive your anxiety, even though it is in fact extremely insulting to me. It most certainly is! Of course it's insulting to think I should be afraid of the vindictive ravings of some pathetic hack. But I do forgive you, because your concern is very attractive and it proves how much you love me. (*Takes her in his arms.*) That's just as it should be, Nora, my love. No matter what. If anything goes wrong, I'll have the courage and strength to deal with it, you can rely on that. Whatever happens, I'll be able to face it by myself, you'll see.

NORA: (*Horror-struck*) What do you mean?

HELMER: What I say.

NORA: (*Firmly*) You'll never ever have to do that.

HELMER: You're right. We'll face it together, Nora . . . as man and wife. That's just as it should be. (*Caresses her.*) Now, are you all right? Come on, you look like a frightened dove. It's all in your imagination, you know, there's nothing to it at all. Now, what you ought to do is rehearse the tarantella again and practise your tambourine a bit. I'll go into the inner office and close the door, so I shan't hear a thing, you can make as much noise as you like. (*Turns in the doorway.*) Tell Rank where to find me when he arrives, will you?

(*He nods to her and exits with his papers into his room, closing the door behind him.* NORA *stands, as if nailed to the floor, bewildered and terrified.*)

NORA: (*Whispering*) He can do it, now. He will do it. Nothing can stop him doing it . . . No, he mustn't, ever! Anything else, but not that! Must find some help. Some way out of it. (*The bell rings.*)

Dr Rank! Any way. Any way will do.

(*She passes her hands over her face, pulls herself together, goes over and opens the hall door.* DR RANK *is outside, hanging up his fur coat. It is beginning to get dark.*)

Good afternoon, Dr Rank. I knew it was you by the way you rang. Don't go in and see Torvald just yet. I think he's busy at the moment.

RANK: What about you?

(*He enters the room, closing the door behind him.*)

NORA: You know very well, I always have time for you.

RANK: Thank you. I'll make use of it as long as I can.

NORA: What do you mean? As long as you can?

RANK: What I say. Do you find it frightening?

NORA: Well, it seems such a strange way of putting it. Are you expecting something to happen?

RANK: I've been expecting something to happen for a long time. And it's about to. I never thought it would be so soon.

NORA: (*Clutching his arm*) What have you found out? Dr Rank, you must tell me!

RANK: (*Sitting down by the fire*) I'm slipping downhill. There's nothing I can do about it.

NORA: (*Sighing with relief*) Oh, that's it, you . . .

RANK: Yes, that's it. It's no good lying to yourself. I'm the most miserable patient on my books, Mrs Helmer. These last few days, I've been totting up my spiritual balance sheet. Bankrupt. In a month's time I'll be lying rotting in the graveyard.

NORA: Really, what a disgusting thing to say.

RANK: It's a fairly disgusting situation. And the worst thing about it is that before it's all over, it's going to get even more disgusting. There's only one more test to be made, and when I've finished that, I shall know more or less when to expect to start falling to pieces. Now, there's something I want to tell you. I know how sensitive Helmer is, I know he has a marked aversion to anything ugly. I don't want him to come and see me . . .

NORA: Oh, but, Dr Rank . . .

RANK: I won't have him there. Not under any circumstances. I'll lock my door to him. As soon as I'm quite sure of the worst, I'll send you a visiting card with a black cross on it, then you'll know that decay and destruction have set in.

NORA: You really are being quite ridiculous today. And I was so hoping you'd be in a good mood.

RANK: I am dying, after all . . . Fancy having to pay like this for someone else's sins. There's no justice in it, is there? And yet one way or another every family seems to suffer from some kind of implacable retribution . . .

NORA: (*Covering her ears*) Oh, that's all nonsense. Now cheer up!

RANK: Well, I suppose the only thing one can do is laugh at it all. Poor, innocent spine, it's got to burn for all my father's carefree army days.

NORA: (*At the table, left*) He had a weakness for asparagus and pâté de foie gras, wasn't that it?

RANK: Yes. And truffles.

NORA: Oh, yes, truffles, that's right. And wasn't it oysters as well?

RANK: Ah, oysters, oysters, needless to say.

NORA: And all that port and champagne. Isn't is sad that all those delicious things should attack the spine?

RANK: Especially when the unfortunate spine they choose to attack has never had any benefit from them.

NORA: Oh, yes, that's the saddest thing of all.

RANK: (*Looking searchingly at her*) Hm . . .

NORA: (*After a pause*) What were you smiling at?

RANK: No, it was you, you were laughing.

NORA: No, I wasn't, it was you, Dr Rank, you were smiling.

RANK: (*Getting up*) I see you're even more cunning than I thought you were.

NORA: I feel rather mad today.

RANK: Apparently.

NORA: (*Putting her hands on his shoulders*) Dear Dr Rank, you're not to die and leave Torvald and me.

RANK: Oh, you'll get over it easily enough. Those who leave are soon forgotten.

NORA: (*Seeing the fear in his eyes*) Do you think so?

RANK: People make new friendships and . . .

NORA: What new friendships?

RANK: You and Helmer both will, when I'm not here. I'd say you were well on the way already. What was that Mrs Linde doing here yesterday?

NORA: Oh, don't say you're jealous of poor Kristine?

RANK: Of course I am. She's going to be my successor in this house. When I'm dead and buried, she'll probably be . . .

NORA: Ssh. Don't talk so loud. She's in there.

RANK: Here again today? You see what I mean.

NORA: She's just helping me sew my costume. Good heavens, you are being unreasonable, aren't you? (*Sits down on the sofa.*) Now do behave yourself, Dr Rank. Tomorrow you'll see how beautifully I shall dance, and you must imagine I'm doing it just for you . . . and, of course, Torvald. Obviously. (*Takes a few things out of the box.*) Sit here, Dr Rank, and I'll show you something.

RANK: (*Sitting down*) What's that?

NORA: There. Look.

RANK: Silk stockings.

NORA: Flesh-coloured. Aren't they lovely? It's too dark now really, but tomorrow . . . Uh, uh, you're only allowed to look at the foot. Well, I suppose I can show you the rest of them.

RANK: Hm . . .

NORA: Why are you looking so critical? Do you think they wouldn't fit me, is that it?

RANK: I'm afraid I'm in no position to form a reliable opinion on the subject.

NORA: (*Looking at him for a moment*) Shame on you. (*Hits him lightly on the ear with the stockings.*) That'll teach you. (*She puts them away again.*)

RANK: What other delights have you in store for me?

NORA: I'm not going to show you anything else. Not if you're going to be so naughty. (*She hums a little, rummaging through her things. Silence.*)

RANK: Sitting here chatting to you like this, I don't know . . . I mean, I just can't imagine what would have become of me if I'd never come to this house.

NORA: (*Smiling*) Yes, I think you really do feel at home here.

RANK: (*Quieter, looking straight in front of him*) And then to have to abandon it all . . .

NORA: Don't talk nonsense. You're not going to abandon anything.

RANK: (*As before*) . . . and not to be able to leave behind some paltry token of gratitude, hardly even a brief regret . . . nothing but an empty place to be filled by the first person who comes along.

NORA: Suppose I were to ask you for . . .? No, never mind . . .

RANK: For what?

NORA: For some great proof of your friendship . . .

RANK: Go on.

NORA: No, I mean . . . a really enormous favour . . .

RANK: Would you really make me so happy, just for once?

NORA: But you don't know what it is yet.

RANK: Well, tell me.

NORA: No, I can't, Dr Rank. It's not fair to ask you for so much. It's not just a favour, it's help and advice and all sorts of things.

RANK: So much the better. I've no idea what it can be. Tell me. Don't you trust me?

NORA: Of course I do, more than anyone. You're my best and most faithful friend, I know you are. So I will tell you. Well, Dr Rank . . . it's something you must help me prevent. Now you know how deeply Torvald loves me, it's impossible to describe how much, he'd never hesitate for a second to give his life for me.

RANK: (*Leaning towards her*) Nora . . . do you think he's the only one . . .?

NORA: (*With a slight start*) What?

RANK: Who would gladly give his life for you?

NORA: (*Sadly*) Oh.

RANK: I swore to myself I'd tell you before I went away. There'll never be a better opportunity. Now you know, Nora. And you know that, more than anyone else, you can safely confide in me.

NORA: (*Getting up, evenly and calmly*) Let me pass, would you? (RANK *lets her pass, but remains seated.*)

RANK: Nora . . .

NORA: (*At the hall door*) Helene, bring in the lamp . . . (*Moves over to the stove.*) Oh, Dr Rank, that was a really terrible thing to do.

RANK: (*Getting up*) To have loved you just as much as anyone else? Is that so terrible?

NORA: No, but to have told me. That was quite unnecessary . . .

RANK: What do you mean? Did you already know . . .? (*The* MAID *comes in with the lamp, puts it on the table and goes out again.*) Nora . . . Mrs Helmer . . . I'm asking you, did you already know?

NORA: Oh, how should I know whether I knew or not? I couldn't tell you . . . How could you be so clumsy, Dr Rank? Just when everything was going so well.

RANK: At least you can be sure now that I'm at your service, body and soul. So say what you were going to say.

NORA: (*Looking at him*) After that?

RANK: Please tell me what it is you want.

NORA: I can't tell you anything now.

RANK: Yes, you can. You mustn't punish me like this. I'll do anything for you that's humanly possible.

NORA: You can't do anything for me now. Anyway, I probably won't need any help. You'll see, the whole thing is probably a figment of my imagination. I'm sure it is, it's bound to be. (*Sits down in the rocking chair and looks at him, smiling.*) You really are a nice man, Dr Rank. Aren't you ashamed of yourself, now the lamp's been brought in?

RANK: No. I'm not. Perhaps I ought to go now. And not come back.

NORA: No, you mustn't do that. You must go on coming here just as you always have. You know very well Torvald can't manage without you.

RANK: Yes, but what about you?

NORA: Oh, I've always enjoyed your visits enormously.

RANK: Yes, and that's what gave me the wrong impression. You've always been rather a mystery to me. I mean, I've often thought you liked being with me almost as much as you liked being with Helmer.

NORA: Yes, well, don't you understand, there are people you love most, but there are other people you almost prefer being with?

RANK: Yes, I suppose there's something in that.

NORA: When I lived at home, obviously I loved Daddy most. But I always thought it was terrific fun to creep off down to the servants' quarters. For one thing, they never preached at me and, for another, the way they used to talk among themselves was so amusing.

RANK: Ah, so I've taken their place, have I?

NORA: (*Jumping up and going over to him*) Oh, no, Dr Rank dear, I didn't mean it like that. But I'm sure you understand that with Torvald it's just like it was with Daddy.

(*The* MAID *enters from the hall.*)

MAID: Excuse me, madam.

(*She whispers to* NORA *and hands her a card.* NORA *glances at it.*)

NORA: Oh!

(*She pushes the card in her pocket.*)

RANK: Something the matter?

NORA: No, nothing, no. It's just it's my new costume . . .

RANK: What? I thought that was your costume there.

NORA: Yes, no, this is another one, one I've ordered. . . . Torvald's not to know about it.

RANK: Oh, I see, so that's the great secret, is it?

NORA: Yes, that's right. Go in and see him, will you, he's in the inner office. And keep him there as long as . . .

RANK: Now calm down. I shan't let him get away.

(*He goes into Helmer's study.*)

NORA: (*To the* MAID) He's waiting in the kitchen, is he?

MAID: Yes, he came up the back stairs.

NORA: But didn't you tell him there was someone here?

MAID: Yes, but it was no good.

NORA: Did he refuse to go?

MAID: Yes, he won't go until he's spoken to you.

NORA: All right, let him come in. But be quiet about it. You mustn't tell anyone about this, Helene, it's a surpirse for my husband . . .

MAID: No, all right, I understand . . .
(*She exits.*)

NORA: It's going to happen. Catastrophe. It's going to happen, after all. No. It mustn't. It can't.
(*She crosses the room and bolts Helmer's door. The* MAID *shows in* KROGSTAD *and closes the door behind him. He is wearing a fur coat, high boots and a fur hat.*)
(*Moving towards him*) Keep your voice down. My husband's in there.

KROGSTAD: I don't care where he is.

NORA: What do you want?

KROGSTAD: Information.

NORA: Well, what is it? Hurry up.

KROGSTAD: I suppose you know I've been dismissed.

NORA: I couldn't stop it, Mr Krogstad. I fought for you as hard as I could, but it was no good.

KROGSTAD: Doesn't your husband love you at all? He knows I can denounce you and yet he still has the face to . . .

NORA: Do you really think I've told him?

KROGSTAD: Well, no, to tell you the truth, I didn't think you had. Good old Torvald Helmer, it wouldn't be like him at all to show so much virility.

NORA: Mr Krogstad, if you're going to talk about my husband, please show some respect.

KROGSTAD: Oh, I respect him, good heavens, yes. But now since you're so carefully keeping this secret, I can only assume that since yesterday you've found out a little more about the exact implications of what you've done.

NORA: Yes, more than you could ever teach me.

KROGSTAD: Oh, well, of course, I'm such a hopeless lawyer . . .

NORA: What is it you want?

KROGSTAD: Just to see how you are, Mrs Helmer. I've been thinking about you all day. You see, even debt collectors and hack journalists and . . . people like me still have some traces of what we call feelings.

NORA: Then show some. Think of my children.

KROGSTAD: Have you or your husband ever thought of mine? Not that it matters. All I wanted to say was that you needn't take all this too seriously. I'm not intending to lay any charges against you for the time being.

NORA: No. I didn't think you would.

KROGSTAD: There's no need for anyone to know about it, the whole thing can be settled quite amicably between the three of us.

NORA: But my husband must never find out about it.

KROGSTAD: How do you propose to stop him finding out? Perhaps you're now in a position to pay me the balance?

NORA: No, not right away.

KROGSTAD: Or perhaps you've some way of raising the money over the next few days?

NORA: No way I'd care to use.

KROGSTAD: In any case, it wouldn't be much good to you. However much money you offered me, you'd never get me to part with that contract.

NORA: What use is it to you, can you explain that?

KROGSTAD: I just want to keep it . . . to have it in my hand. No outsider will know anything about it. So if you were considering some desperate plan . . .

NORA: I am.

KROGSTAD: . . . like running away from home . . .

NORA: I am!

KROGSTAD: . . . or something worse than that . . .

NORA: How do you know that?

KROGSTAD: . . . forget it.

NORA: How do you know what I'm thinking?

KROGSTAD: Most of us think about that at the beginning. I did. But I didn't have the courage . . .

NORA: (*Tonelessly*) Neither have I.

KROGSTAD: (*Relieved*) No, you haven't the courage either, have you?

NORA: No, I haven't. I haven't.

KROGSTAD: Anyway, it would be an extremely stupid thing to do. All that'll happen is a slight domestic crisis, and then . . . I have a letter to your husband in my pocket.

NORA: Telling him about it?

KROGSTAD: As euphemistically as possible.

NORA: (*Quickly*) He mustn't read that letter. Tear it up. I will get hold of the money somehow.

KROGSTAD: I'm sorry, Mrs Helmer, I thought I'd just explained to you . . .

NORA: No, I'm not talking about the money I owe you. Tell me how much you want from my husband and I'll find it.

KROGSTAD: I don't want money from your husband.

NORA: Then what do you want?

KROGSTAD: I'll tell you, shall I, Mrs Helmer? I want to get back and I want to get on. And your husband's going to help me. I've been there a year and a half now and I've been a model employee. The whole time I've been struggling along in the most abject poverty. But I was quite happy to work my way up step by step. Not any more though, not since I was kicked out: it's not enough for me any more, just to be given my job back as a great favour. As I said, I want to get on. I want promotion. Your husband will have to create a new post for me . . .

NORA: He'd never do that!

KROGSTAD: Oh, yes, he would. I know him. He wouldn't dare raise a murmur. And once we're working together, you'll see what'll happen. Within a year I'll be the manager's right-hand man. It'll be Nils Krogstad, not Torvald Helmer, running the Joint Stock Bank.

NORA: You'll never manage it.

KROGSTAD: Well, you're not going to . . .

NORA: I do have the courage now.

KROGSTAD: Oh, you can't frighten me. A spoiled, sensitive lady like you . . .

NORA: You'll see. You'll see!

KROGSTAD: Under the ice, will it be? Down into the cold, pitch-black water? Floating to the surface next spring, bloated, hairless, unrecognizable . . .

NORA: You can't frighten me.

KROGSTAD: And you can't frighten me either. People don't do things like that, Mrs Helmer. Anyway, what use would it be? I'd still have your husband exactly where I wanted him.

NORA: What, afterwards? Even if I . . .?

KROGSTAD: You forget that I own your reputation.

(NORA *stands speechless, staring at him.*)

Well, now you know. So don't do anything stupid. When Helmer's read my letter, I expect an answer from him. And remember, it's your husband who's forced me back on this path. I'll never forgive him for that. Goodbye, Mrs Helmer. (*He exits into the hall.* NORA *goes over to the door, opens it slightly and listens.*)

NORA: He's going. He's not going to deliver the letter. No, that's impossible. (*Opens the door wider.*) What's happening? He's just standing there. He's waiting at the top of the stairs. Perhaps he's reconsidering. Perhaps . . .

(*A letter falls into the letterbox.* KROGSTAD'S *footsteps, gradually retreating down the stairs.* NORA *suppresses a scream and rushes across to the table by the sofa. Pause.*)

In the letterbox. (*Creeps back to the hall door.*) There it is. Torvald, Torvald. That's the end of us.

(MRS LINDE *enters from the left with the costume.*)

MRS LINDE: Yes, well, that would seem to be that. Would you like to try it on . . .?

NORA: (*Quietly and hoarsely*) Come here, Kristine.

MRS LINDE: (*Throwing the costume on to the sofa*) What's the matter? You look quite distraught.

NORA: Come here. Do you see that letter? There, look, through the glass of the letterbox.

MRS LINDE: Yes.

NORA: That letter's from Krogstad . . .

MRS LINDE: Nora . . . it was Krogstad who lent you the money, wasn't it?

NORA: Yes. And now Torvald's going to find out everything.

MRS LINDE: Believe me, Nora, it's the best thing for both of you.

NORA: It's worse than you think. I forged a name.

MRS LINDE: But . . .?

NORA: Now there's just one thing I want to ask you, Kristine, I want you to be my witness.

MRS LINDE: Witness? What do you mean?

NORA: If I were to have a breakdown, which might easily happen . . .

MRS LINDE: Nora!

NORA: Or if something else were to happen to me . . . something that might prevent me from being here . . .

MRS LINDE: Whatever's the matter with you, Nora?

NORA: And someone tried to take all the blame on themselves, you understand me . . .

MRS LINDE: Yes, but you're not thinking of . . .?

NORA: You'll be my witness that it isn't true, won't you, Kristine? There's nothing the matter with me, I know exactly what I'm saying, and I'm telling you, no one else has ever known anything about this, I did it all myself, everything. Remember that.

MRS LINDE: I will. But I don't understand it at all.

NORA: How could you understand it? Or that the miracle is about to happen.

MRS LINDE: Miracle?

NORA: Yes, the miracle. But it's so terrifying, Kristine. We mustn't let it happen, not for anything.

MRS LINDE: I'll go round and speak to Krogstad now.

NORA: Don't. He'll try to harm you as well.

MRS LINDE: There was a time when he would have done anything for me.

NORA: What?

MRS LINDE: Where does he live?

NORA: Oh, I don't know . . . wait a minute . . . (*Puts her hand in her pocket.*) Here's his card. But what about the letter . . .?

HELMER: (*In the study, knocking on the door*) Nora!

NORA: (*Crying out in terror*) Oh, what is it? What do you want?

HELMER: All right, no need to sound so frightened, we can't come in, you've locked the door. Are you trying something on?

NORA: Yes, I'm just . . . trying something on. I'm going to look so pretty, Torvald.

MRS LINDE: (*Having read the card*) He lives just round the corner.

NORA: Yes, but it's no good. We're finished. That letter's out there in the letterbox.

MRS LINDE: And does your husband have the key?

NORA: Always.

MRS LINDE: Krogstad must ask for his letter back, he'll have to think of some excuse . . .

NORA: But it's about now Torvald usually . . .

MRS LINDE: Stop him. Go in and talk to him for a bit. I'll be back as quickly as I can.

(*She exits quickly by the hall door.* NORA *goes over to Helmer's door, opens it and peeps in.*)

NORA: Torvald.

HELMER: (*In his study*) Well, at last, may I please have permission to come into my own room now? Come along, Rank, now we'll see something . . . (*Appears in the doorway.*) What's going on?

NORA: What do you mean, Torvald?

HELMER: Well, Rank promised me some extraordinary transformation scene.

RANK: (*In the doorway*) I must have misunderstood.

NORA: Yes, no one's going to see me in all my glory until tomorrow.

HELMER: But, Nora, what's the matter? You look so exhausted. Have you been doing too much practice?

NORA: No, I haven't done any practice at all.

HELMER: You'll have to, you know . . .

NORA: Yes, I know I'll have to, Torvald. But I won't get anywhere unless you help me, I've completely forgotten everything.

HELMER: Oh, we'll soon refresh your memory.

148

NORA: Yes, look after me, Torvald. Will you promise? I'm so nervous. That great big party. This evening you must devote yourself entirely to me. No distractions, no work, you mustn't even pick up a pen. Mm? Do you promise, Torvald?

HELMER: I promise. I shall be completely at your disposal the whole evening. Erm, there's just one thing I . . .
(*He moves towards the hall door.*)

NORA: Where are you going?

HELMER: I'm just going to see if there's any mail.

NORA: No, Torvald, don't!

HELMER: Why not?

NORA: Please, Torvald, please, there isn't any.

HELMER: I'm just going to have a look.
(*He is on his way out.* NORA *goes to the piano and plays the opening bars of the tarantella.* HELMER *pauses in the doorway.*) Ah!

NORA: I can't dance tomorrow, if you don't let me rehearse.
(HELMER *goes over to her.*)

HELMER: Poor Nora, are you really so nervous?

NORA: Yes, terribly nervous. I want to rehearse now, there's still time before dinner. Please sit down and play for me, Torvald. I want you to direct me and tell me what to do, like you always used to.

HELMER: All right, of course, if that's what you want, I'd be only too pleased.
(*He sits at the piano.* NORA *takes her tambourine out of the box, as well as a long, multicoloured shawl, which she quickly drapes round her shoulders. Then she jumps forward into the middle of the room.*)

NORA: Now, play for me. I want to dance.
(HELMER *plays and* NORA *dances.* DR RANK *stands at the piano behind* HELMER *and watches.*)

HELMER: (*Playing*) Not so fast . . . not so fast.

NORA: I can't help it.

HELMER: It's too violent, Nora!

NORA: It has to be.

HELMER: (*Stopping*) No, no, no, this is no good at all.

149

NORA: (*Laughing and flourishing the tambourine*) I told you, didn't I?

RANK: I'll play for her, shall I?

HELMER: (*Getting up*) Yes, do, then it'll be easier for me to direct her.

(RANK *sits at the piano and plays.* NORA *dances with increasing frenzy.* HELMER *stands by the stove, issuing constant instructions, which she appears not to hear. Her hair works loose and falls down over her shoulders. She takes no notice and goes on dancing.* MRS LINDE *enters and stands transfixed in the doorway.*)

MRS LINDE: Oh . . .!

NORA: (*As she dances*) We're enjoying ourselves, Kristine.

HELMER: My dear Nora, you're dancing as if your life depended on it.

NORA: It does.

HELMER: Rank, stop, will you? This is absolute madness. Stop, I said.

(RANK *stops playing and* NORA *comes to a sudden halt.* HELMER *goes across to her.*)

I can't believe it. You've forgotten everything I taught you.

NORA: (*Throwing the tambourine aside*) I told you.

HELMER: Well, we'll have to do something about that, won't we?

NORA: Yes, you can see how much it's needed. You'll have to rehearse me right up to the last minute. Do you promise me, Torvald?

HELMER: You can rely on me.

NORA: Today and tomorrow you're not to think of anything but me. You're not to open a letter . . . you're not even to look in the letterbox . . .

HELMER: You're still worrying about that man . . .

NORA: Yes, well, there is that as well.

HELMER: Nora, I can see it in your face, there's a letter from him out there.

NORA: I don't know. I think there is. But you're not to read anything more now. You're not to let anything as ugly as that come between us until all this is over.

RANK: (*Quietly to* HELMER) You mustn't contradict her.

HELMER: (*Putting his arm round her*) All right, my little girl shall have her own way. But tomorrow night, when you've danced your dance . . .

NORA: You'll be free.

(*The* MAID *appears in the doorway, right.*)

MAID: Dinner is served now, madam.

NORA: Bring some champagne, Helene.

MAID: Yes, madam.

(*She exits.*)

HELMER: Oh, I see, we're celebrating, are we?

NORA: Yes, we're celebrating and drinking champagne till dawn. And a few macaroons, Helene, lots of macaroons . . . just for once.

HELMER: (*Taking her hand*) Now then, that's enough excitement. Where's my little lark? She never used to behave like this.

NORA: I know, I'll behave now. Go on in now. And you, Dr Rank. Kristine, help me put my hair up, will you?

RANK: (*Quietly, on the way out*) She's not, erm, you know, she isn't, is she?

HELMER: No, no, no, nothing like that. It's what I was saying to you. She's like a child when she gets nervous.

(*They exit, right.*)

NORA: Well?

MRS LINDE: He's left for the country.

NORA: I could tell by your face.

MRS LINDE: He's coming back tomorrow evening. I've left a message for him.

NORA: You shouldn't have. You won't stop it happening. And really there's something exhilarating about it, isn't there, waiting for the miracle.

MRS LINDE: What is it you're waiting for?

NORA: Oh, you wouldn't understand. Go in and join them. I'll be with you in a minute.

(MRS LINDE *goes off to the dining room.* NORA *stands for a moment, as though collecting her thoughts. Then she looks at her watch.*)

Five. Seven hours to midnight. Then twenty-four hours to midnight tomorrow. Then the tarantella will be over. Twenty-four and seven. Thirty-one hours to live.

(HELMER *appears in the doorway, right.*)

HELMER: Where's my little lark?

NORA: (*Running to him with open arms*) Here she is!

ACT THREE

The same room. The table and the chairs around it have been moved forward to the middle of the room. There is a lighted lamp on the table. The hall door is open. Dance music can be heard from the floor above.
    MRS LINDE *is sitting at the table, leafing absently through a book. She is trying to read, but seems unable to concentrate. Now and then she looks up at the door, listening anxiously.*

MRS LINDE: (*Looking at her watch*) Still not here. There's not much time left. If only he'd . . . (*She listens again.*) Ah, that must be him.
    (*She goes into the hall and cautiously opens the front door. Quiet footsteps on the stairs. She whispers.*)
    Come in. There's no one here.
KROGSTAD: (*In the doorway*) I found a message from you at home. What's all this about?
MRS LINDE: I must talk to you.
KROGSTAD: Oh? And must you talk to me in this house?
MRS LINDE: It's impossible where I'm staying. There's no private entrance to my room. Come in. We're quite alone. The servants are asleep and the Helmers are upstairs, at the ball.
KROGSTAD: (*Coming into the living room*) Oh, so the Helmers are out dancing this evening, are they?
MRS LINDE: Why shouldn't they be?
KROGSTAD: Why indeed?
MRS LINDE: Well, Krogstad, it's time for us to have a talk.
KROGSTAD: Have we anything to talk about?
MRS LINDE: A great deal.
KROGSTAD: I wouldn't have thought so.
MRS LINDE: No, that's because you never really understood me.
KROGSTAD: What was there to understand about it? It's the oldest story in the world. An unscrupulous woman sending a man packing when something a bit more profitable comes along.

MRS LINDE: Do you really think I'm that unscrupulous? Do you think I broke it off just like that?

KROGSTAD: Well, didn't you?

MRS LINDE: Is that what you really think?

KROGSTAD: If it isn't true, why did you write me that letter?

MRS LINDE: I had no choice. If I had to break with you, I felt it was only right to try to destroy your feelings for me.

KROGSTAD: (*Clenching his fists*) So that was it. And all that just . . . just for money.

MRS LINDE: You must remember I had a helpless mother and two young brothers to take care of. We couldn't wait for you. Your prospects did seem rather shaky at the time.

KROGSTAD: That's as may be. You still had no right to reject me for someone else.

MRS LINDE: I don't know. I've often wondered whether or not I had the right.

KROGSTAD: (*Quietly*) When I lost you, it was as if all the firm ground had crumbled beneath my feet. Look at me now, I'm like a shipwrecked man.

MRS LINDE: Perhaps you'll be rescued soon.

KROGSTAD: I was about to be. Until you came along and prevented it.

MRS LINDE: Quite involuntarily. I only found out today that it was you I was to replace at the bank.

KROGSTAD: I believe you. But now you do know, you're not going to do anything about it, are you?

MRS LINDE: No. Even if I did, it wouldn't be any help to you.

KROGSTAD: Help, help, I would have done it anyway.

MRS LINDE: Well, I've learnt to be sensible. The hard and bitter necessities of life have taught me that.

KROGSTAD: And life has taught me not to trust high-minded platitudes.

MRS LINDE: Then you've learnt something very sensible. But you still trust actions, don't you?

KROGSTAD: What do you mean?

MRS LINDE: You said you felt like a shipwrecked man.

KROGSTAD: I had good reason to.

MRS LINDE: Well, I feel like a shipwrecked woman. Nothing to look back on and no one to look after.

KROGSTAD: It was your decision.

MRS LINDE: It was the only decision I could make.

KROGSTAD: Well, what about it?

MRS LINDE: If two shipwrecked people join hands . . .

KROGSTAD: What?

MRS LINDE: . . . don't you think they stand a better chance of being rescued?

KROGSTAD: Kristine!

MRS LINDE: Why do you think I came to town?

KROGSTAD: You couldn't have been thinking about me?

MRS LINDE: I have to work, or I find life unbearable. All my life, as far back as I can remember, I've worked, and it's been the only real happiness I've had. But now I'm all alone in the world, it's terrible, I feel so lost and hollow. There's no happiness left in working for yourself. Give me someone and something to work for, Krogstad.

KROGSTAD: I don't believe it. It's just some romantic female instinct for noble self-sacrifice.

MRS LINDE: Have you ever known me to be romantic?

KROGSTAD: You can't really mean it. Tell me . . . do you know about my past?

MRS LINDE: Yes.

KROGSTAD: And my reputation?

MRS LINDE: I thought you said that with me you would have been a different person.

KROGSTAD: I'm sure I would have been.

MRS LINDE: Isn't there still time?

KROGSTAD: Kristine . . . you've thought about this carefully, haven't you? I can see you have. Have you really got the courage . . . ?

MRS LINDE: I need someone to look after, and your children need a mother. You and I need each other. I have faith in you, Krogstad. I'd risk anything for you.

KROGSTAD: (*Gripping her hands*) Thank you, Kristine, thank you. Now I'll be able to find a way to redeem myself in people's eyes. Oh, I'd forgotten . . .

MRS LINDE: (*Listening*) Ssh! It's the tarantella. You must go.

KROGSTAD: Why? What do you mean?

MRS LINDE: Can you hear the music up there? When it's finished, they'll be coming down.

KROGSTAD: All right, I'll go. It's all over, anyway. You don't know what I've done to the Helmers, do you?

MRS LINDE: I do know, yes.

KROGSTAD: And you still had the courage to . . . ?

MRS LINDE: I understand how far a man like you can be driven by despair.

KROGSTAD: If I could only undo it.

MRS LINDE: You can. Your letter's still in the letterbox.

KROGSTAD: Are you sure?

MRS LINDE: Quite sure. But . . .

KROGSTAD: (*Looking hard at her*) Is that what all this means? Rescuing your friend at any price? You might as well tell me. Is that it?

MRS LINDE: A woman who has sold herself once for the sake of others doesn't make the same mistake again.

KROGSTAD: I'll demand my letter back.

MRS LINDE: No, no.

KROGSTAD: Yes, of course, that's what I'll do. I'll wait here till Helmer comes down. Then I'll ask him to give me back my letter . . . I'll say it's just about my dismissal and that I'd rather he didn't read it . . .

MRS LINDE: No, Krogstad. Don't ask for your letter back.

KROGSTAD: But wasn't that why you originally asked me to come up here?

MRS LINDE: Yes, in the panic of the moment. But there's been a whole day since then and in that time I've seen extraordinary things in this house. Helmer must find out about everything. All this unhealthy secrecy must stop and then they'll be able to come to a full understanding of each other. They can't go on in this atmosphere of deceit and intrigue.

KROGSTAD: Well, if you think the risk is worth taking . . .

anyway, at least there's one thing I can do for them straight
away . . .

MRS LINDE: (*Listening*) Hurry! Go, you must go! The dance is
finished. They'll be here any minute.

KROGSTAD: I'll wait for you outside.

MRS LINDE: Yes, do. I want you to see me home.

KROGSTAD: I've never been so happy in my life.

(*He goes out the front door, leaving the hall door open.* MRS
LINDE *tidies up a bit and gets her overcoat, ready to go.*)

MRS LINDE: It's wonderful. Wonderful. Someone to work for . . .
and to live for. A happy home to build. That's something
really worth doing . . . I wish they'd come. (*Listens.*) That
must be them. I must get ready.

(*She picks up her hat and coat. The voices of* HELMER *and*
NORA *are heard outside. A key is turned in the lock and*
HELMER *leads* NORA, *almost by force, into the hall. She is
wearing her Italian costume with a large black shawl round her
shoulders. He is in evening dress with an open black domino.*)

NORA: (*Struggling in the doorway*) No, no, I'm not going in! I want
to go back upstairs, I don't want to leave so early.

HELMER: But, Nora, my dear . . .

NORA: Oh, please, Torvald, please, if I ask you nicely, just for an
hour or so . . .

HELMER: Not another minute, Nora. You know what we agreed.
Now, come along in, you'll catch cold standing here.

(*In spite of her resistance, he leads her gently into the room.*)

MRS LINDE: Good evening.

NORA: Kristine!

HELMER: Ah, Mrs Linde, you round here at this time of night?

MRS LINDE: Yes, forgive me. I did want to see Nora in her
costume.

NORA: Have you been sitting here waiting for me?

MRS LINDE: Yes. Unfortunately, I arrived too late, you'd already
gone up. And I thought I couldn't leave without having seen
you.

HELMER: (*Taking off* NORA'*s shawl*) Well, there you are. She's
certainly worth looking at. Lovely, isn't she, Mrs Linde?

MRS LINDE: Yes, I must admit . . .

HELMER: Exceptionally lovely, isn't she? Everyone at the party thought so. She's a dear little thing, but she's so terribly stubborn. What are we going to do with her? I almost had to drag her away, if you can imagine.

NORA: Oh, Torvald, you'll be sorry you grudged me another half hour there.

HELMER: You see what I mean, Mrs Linde? She danced the tarantella and she was a tumultuous success . . . which she deserved to be, although there was a little too much realism in her performance, I mean to say, more than was perhaps strictly speaking required by the demands of art. However, that's by the way. The main thing is she was a success, a . . . tumultuous success. Now, should I have let her stay after that? And dissipate the effect? No fear. I took my lovely little girl from Capri . . . or perhaps I should say my *capricious* little girl from Capri . . . I took her by the arm. A quick spin round the room, goodnight everybody, and then, as they say in all those novels, the beautiful vision melted away. Exits should always be effective, Mrs Linde, but I can't seem to get that into Nora's head. Foo, it's warm in here. (*Throws his domino on to a chair and opens the door to his study.*) Why is it dark in here? Oh, yes, of course. Excuse me . . .
(*He goes into his study and lights some candles.*)

NORA: (*A breathless whisper*) Well?

MRS LINDE: (*Quickly*) I've spoken to him.

NORA: And?

MRS LINDE: Nora . . . you must tell your husband everything.

NORA: (*Tonelessly*) I knew it.

MRS LINDE: You have nothing to fear from Krogstad now. But you must tell him all the same.

NORA: I'm not going to.

MRS LINDE: Then the letter will.

NORA: Thank you, Kristine. Now I know what I have to do. Ssh . . . !

HELMER: (*Returning*) Well, Mrs Linde, have you had time to admire her?

MRS LINDE: Yes. I must say goodnight now.

HELMER: What, already? Is this your knitting?

MRS LINDE: (*Taking it*) Yes, it is, thank you, I'd almost forgotten it.

HELMER: You like knitting, then, do you?

MRS LINDE: Yes, I do.

HELMER: You know something, you'd prefer embroidery.

MRS LINDE: Would I?

HELMER: Oh, yes, it's so much prettier to watch. Look. You hold the embroidery in your left hand, like this, and then you take the needle in your right hand, like that, and you bring it up in a long, graceful curve. See?

MRS LINDE: Yes, I suppose so . . .

HELMER: Whereas knitting can never look anything but ugly. Can it? Arms clamped in to your sides and the needles bobbing up and down . . . there's something Chinese about it. Excellent champagne they were serving.

MRS LINDE: Well, goodnight, Nora, don't be stubborn any more.

HELMER: Well said, Mrs Linde.

MRS LINDE: Goodnight, Mr Helmer.

HELMER: (*Showing her to the door*) Goodnight, goodnight. I hope you'll be all right to get home. I'd be delighted to – er . . . but you haven't got very far to go, have you? Goodnight, goodnight. (*She goes. He shuts the door behind her and comes back into the room.*) At last! I thought we'd never get rid of her. She's a terrible bore, that woman.

NORA: Aren't you very tired, Torvald?

HELMER: No, not at all.

NORA: Don't you feel sleepy?

HELMER: No, on the contrary, I feel extremely lively. You look very tired, though, and sleepy.

NORA: Yes, I am tired. I'll soon be asleep.

HELMER: There you are, you see, I was right not to let you stay longer.

NORA: You're always right.

HELMER: (*Kissing her on the forehead*) That's more like my little lark. Did you notice how cheerful Rank was this evening?

NORA: No, was he? I didn't talk to him.

HELMER: Neither did I very much. But I haven't seen him in such a good mood for ages. (*Looks at her for a moment, then moves nearer to her.*) It's marvellous to be home again and to be all alone with you. You lovely, fascinating girl.

NORA: Don't look at me like that, Torvald.

HELMER: Why shouldn't I look at my most treasured possession? And think that all that beauty is mine and mine alone, absolutely and completely mine?

NORA: (*Walking round to the other side of the table*) You mustn't say things like that to me tonight.

HELMER: (*Following her*) I see you still have the tarantella in your blood. It makes you even more attractive. Listen. The guests are beginning to leave. (*Softly*) Nora . . . soon the whole house will be quiet.

NORA: I hope so.

HELMER: Yes, of course you do, Nora, my love. Do you know . . . when I go out with you like this to a party . . . do you know why I hardly say anything to you and keep away from you and only steal a glance at you occasionally, do you know why? Because I pretend you're my secret lover, that we're secretly engaged and that no one suspects there's anything between us.

NORA: Yes, I know you're thinking about me all the time.

HELMER: And then, when it's time to go and I put your shawl around your slender young shoulders and the wonderful curve of your neck, I imagine you're my young bride, that we're just arriving from the wedding, that for the first time I'm leading you into my house, and that for the first time I'm alone with you . . . alone with you and all your young and trembling beauty. I've been longing for you all evening. When I saw you dance the predatory temptress of the tarantella . . . my blood boiled. I couldn't bear it any longer. That's why I brought you down here so early . . .

NORA: Stop it, Torvald. You must leave me alone now. I won't have all this.

HELMER: What was that? You're teasing me, aren't you, Nora, aren't you? Won't have all this, won't! After all, I am your husband . . .

(*A knock at the door.*)

NORA: (*Starting*) Did you hear that?

HELMER: (*Moving towards the hall*) Who is it?

RANK: (*Outside*) It's me. May I come in for a minute?

HELMER: (*Quietly, annoyed*) What's he after now? (*Aloud*) Just a second. (*Opens the door.*) Come in, it's very good of you not to pass us by.

RANK: I thought I heard your voice and I just felt like calling in. (*Glances quickly round the room.*) Yes, yes. Dear old familiar room. I do enjoy being with you, it's so comfortable here.

HELMER: You seemed to be enjoying yourself upstairs as well.

RANK: Enormously. And why not? Why shouldn't people take whatever the world offers? As much as they can for as long as they can. The wine was excellent . . .

HELMER: Especially the champagne.

RANK: Ah, you noticed that as well, did you? It's incredible how much I managed to pour down myself.

NORA: Torvald drank a lot of champagne this evening too.

RANK: Did he?

NORA: Yes. It always makes him so cheerful.

RANK: Well, why shouldn't you have a happy evening after a good day's work?

HELMER: A good day's work? I'm afraid I can't claim to have done much today.

RANK: (*Slapping him on the back*) Ah, but you see, I can.

NORA: Dr Rank, you've been conducting a scientific examination today, haven't you?

RANK: That's right.

HELMER: Whatever next? Little Nora talking about scientific examinations!

NORA: And should I congratulate you on the result?

RANK: You certainly should.

NORA: Good, was it?

RANK: The best possible for the doctor and the patient. Certainty.

NORA: (*Quickly and urgently*) Certainty?

RANK: Absolute certainty. So I was right to enjoy myself this evening, wasn't I?

NORA: Yes, you were right, Dr Rank.

HELMER: I agree. As long as you don't suffer for it tomorrow.

RANK: Well, in this life you don't get anything for nothing.

NORA: You like fancy-dress balls, don't you, Dr Rank?

RANK: Yes, when there are a lot of funny disguises . . .

NORA: Listen, what shall we go as next time?

HELMER: Thinking about next time already, what a frivolous little thing you are.

RANK: What shall we go as? I'll tell you, shall I? You'll be fortune's child . . .

HELMER: What sort of costume does she wear?

RANK: Your wife must just appear as she does every day on her way through the world . . .

HELMER: You old phrasemaker. Do you know what you'd go as?

RANK: Oh, yes, I've made up my mind already.

HELMER: Go on.

RANK: At the next fancy-dress ball, I'm going to be invisible.

HELMER: What a bizarre idea.

RANK: There's an enormous black hat, haven't you heard about it, a hat that makes you invisible. You just pull it right down over yourself and no one can see you any more.

HELMER: (*Suppressing a smile*) That's right, of course.

RANK: I don't know, I'd quite forgotten what I came for. Helmer, give me a cigar, will you, one of those dark Havanas.

HELMER: Pleasure, here you are.

(*He hands him the cigar box.* RANK *takes one and clips the end off.*)

RANK: Thanks.

NORA: (*Striking a match*) Let me light it for you.

RANK: Thank you.

(*She holds the match up for him. He lights the cigar.*)

Well, goodbye now.

HELMER: Goodbye, old man.

NORA: Sleep well, Dr Rank.

RANK: Kind wish, thank you.

NORA: Wish me the same.

RANK: You? All right then, if you like . . . Sleep well. And thanks
for the light.

(*He nods to them and goes.*)

HELMER: (*In an undertone*) Drunk.

NORA: (*Absently*) Possibly.

(HELMER *takes his bunch of keys and goes out into the hall.*)
Torvald . . . what are you doing out there?

HELMER: Emptying the letterbox. It's quite full. There'll be no
room for the papers tomorrow morning . . .

NORA: Are you going to work tonight?

HELMER: You know very well I'm not . . . What's this?
Somebody's been at the lock.

NORA: The lock . . . ?

HELMER: I'm sure of it. Who could it have been? I can't think the
servants would . . . There's a broken hairpin here, Nora. It's
one of yours . . .

NORA: (*Hastily*) Must have been the children . . .

HELMER: Then you must put a stop to that sort of behaviour. Now,
let's see . . . there we are, I've managed to get it open. (*Takes
the letters out and calls to the kitchen.*) Helene? Helene. Put out
the lamp in the porch, will you? (*Comes back with the letters in
his hand, shutting the hall door.*) Look. Look how the mail has
piled up. (*Glances through it.*) What's this?

NORA: (*At the window*) A letter! No, Torvald, no!

HELMER: Two visiting cards . . . from Rank.

NORA: From Dr Rank?

HELMER: (*Looking at them*) Dr Rank, that's right. They were on
top. He must have pushed them in as he was leaving.

NORA: Has he written anything on them?

HELMER: There's a black cross above his name. Look. It's rather
sinister, isn't it? Almost as if he were announcing his own death.

NORA: He is.

HELMER: What? Do you know about it? Has he said anything to
you?

NORA: Yes. The cards are his way of saying goodbye to us. He's going to shut himself away and die.

HELMER: Poor chap. I knew he wouldn't be with us very much longer. But so soon . . . and to go and hide himself away like that, like some wounded animal.

NORA: When it has to happen, it's best for it to happen without words. Don't you think, Torvald?

HELMER: (*Pacing up and down*) He'd become so much a part of us, I can't imagine life without him. With his sufferings and his loneliness, he was the cloudy background of our sunlit happiness . . . Well, perhaps it's all for the best. For him, anyway. (*Stands still.*) And maybe for us as well, Nora. Now you and I have nothing but each other to fall back on. (*Puts his arms around her.*) Oh, my dear wife; sometimes I feel I could never hold you close enough. Do you know, Nora, I often wish you were threatened by some impending disaster, so I could risk everything, life and limb, everything, for your sake.

NORA: (*Wrenching herself away and speaking firmly and decisively*) You must read your letters now, Torvald.

HELMER: No, not tonight. Tonight I want to be with you, my dear wife.

NORA: Your friend is dying, how can you think about anything else?

HELMER: You're right. It's upset both of us. Something ugly has come between us. A flavour of death and decay. We must shake free of it and until we do . . . we must each go to our own room.

NORA: (*With her arms around his neck*) Goodnight, Torvald, goodnight!

HELMER: (*Kissing her on the forehead*) Goodnight, my little songbird. Sleep well, Nora. I'm going to read my letters. (*He takes the bundle of letters with him into the study, closing the door behind him.* NORA, *her eyes distraught, gropes around for Helmer's domino, picks it up and throws it round her shoulders, whispering quickly, hoarsely and brokenly.*)

NORA: Never to see him again. Never. Never. Never. (*Puts her*

shawl over her head.) Never to see the children again. Them as well. Never, never . . . Icy, black water. Deep . . . if . . . if only it were over. He's opening it now, he's reading it. No, Torvald, no, not yet, goodbye, goodbye, my children.
(*She begins to run towards the hall. At the same time,* HELMER *throws open his door and stands there holding an opened letter.*)

HELMER: Nora!

NORA: (*Crying out*) Ah . . . !

HELMER: What is this? Do you know what's in this letter?

NORA: Yes, I know. Now, let me go! I'm going!

HELMER: (*Holding her back*) Where?

NORA: (*Trying to break away from him*) You're not going to save me, Torvald!

HELMER: (*Recoiling from her*) So it's true! What he says, true. How terrible! No. No, it can't be true, it's impossible.

NORA: It *is* true. There was nothing in the world I loved more than you.

HELMER: I don't want your idiotic excuses.

NORA: (*Taking a step towards him*) Torvald . . . !

HELMER: Have you any idea of what you've done, you stupid woman!

NORA: Let me go. You mustn't help me. You mustn't take all the blame just for my sake.

HELMER: I don't want any melodramatics. (*Locks the hall door.*) You're staying here until you've given me an explanation. Do you realize what you've done? Answer me! Do you?

NORA: (*Looking at him intently, her expression hardening*) Yes, I'm beginning to realize exactly what I've done.

HELMER: (*Pacing up and down*) This is a rude awakening, I can tell you. For all these years, for eight years now, you've been my pride and joy, and now I find you're a hypocrite and a liar, and worse, worse than that . . . a criminal! The whole thing is an abyss of ugliness! You ought to be ashamed.
(NORA *says nothing and goes on looking intently at him. He stops in front of her*) Of course, I might have known something like this would happen. I should have seen it coming. All your father's fundamental irresponsibility . . . Don't interrupt!

All your father's fundamental irresponsibility has been passed on to you. No religion, no morals, no sense of duty . . . This is my punishment for turning a blind eye to what he did. I did it for your sake – and this is how you repay me.

NORA: That's right.

HELMER: You've destroyed all my happiness. You've ruined my whole future. It doesn't bear thinking about. I'm at the mercy of a totally unscrupulous man. I'm completely in his power, he can make any demands on me he likes, order me about whenever the fancy takes him . . . and I'll have to do what I'm told without a murmur. To think I should have to sink so low because of a woman's irresponsibility.

NORA: When I'm out of the way, you'll be free again.

HELMER: Oh, spare us the grand gestures! That's like your father as well, he was always ready with a glib phrase. Anyway, what good do you suppose it would do me if you were out of the way, as you put it? It wouldn't do me any good at all. He could still tell people about this. And if he does, I might be suspected of having known about your crime all along. Or they might even think that it was my plan and that I encouraged you to do it! And this is what I've got to thank you for, after looking after you so well all through our marriage. Now do you realize what you've done to me?

NORA: (*Calmly and coldly*) Yes.

HELMER: This is all so incredible, I can hardly grasp that it's happened. We shall have to come to some arrangement. Take off your shawl. Take it off, I said! I shall have to find some way of appeasing him. It'll have to be hushed up, however much it costs. As far as you and I are concerned, we shall have to make it look as if nothing has changed between us. Just to keep up appearances, of course. I mean, you'll obviously have to stay on in the house, but you won't be allowed to have anything to do with the children. I can't take the risk . . . Imagine having to say that to someone I loved so much, to someone I still . . . ! That's all over, now. There's no question of being happy any more: it's just picking up the bits and pieces and making some sort of show . . .

(*The doorbell rings.* HELMER *starts.*)

... of it ... Who can that be? So late? It couldn't be ...
could it? You'd better hide, Nora! Say you're not well.
(NORA *doesn't move.* HELMER *goes over and unlocks the hall
door. The* MAID *appears, half dressed.*)

MAID: It's a letter for you, madam.

HELMER: Give it to me. (*Grabs it and closes the door.*) Yes, it's
from him. You're not going to get it. I'll read it myself.

NORA: Do.

HELMER: (*By the lamp*) I hardly dare. This may be the end of us
both. I must look at it. (*Hurriedly tears open the letter, reads a
few lines, looks at a piece of paper enclosed in the letter. Then, a
cry of joy.*) Nora!

(NORA *looks at him, puzzled.*)

Nora! ... Wait a minute, I must read it again ... Yes, it's
true, yes. I'm saved! Nora, I'm saved!

NORA: What about me?

HELMER: Yes, well, and you, obviously. We're both saved, you
and I, both of us. Look. He's sent you back your IOU. He
apologizes, he says he regrets having done what he did, he
says a happy change in his life ... oh, what's it matter what
he says? We're saved, Nora! No one has any proof against
you now. Oh, Nora ... no, first we must get rid of this whole
appalling business. Let's see ... (*Glances at the document.*)
No, I don't want to look at it: from now on all this will be
nothing but a dream. (*Tears up the document and both the
letters, throws them in the oven and watches them burn.*) There,
that's the end of it. He said you'd known about it since
Christmas Eve ... It must have been a terrible three days for
you, Nora.

NORA: It's been a hard struggle, yes, these last three days.

HELMER: And you must have suffered so much, the only way out
you could think of was ... No, let's not bring up all those
horrors again. Let's just be happy and keep telling ourselves
it's over. It's over! Listen to me, Nora. You don't seem to
have grasped it. It's over. Why are you looking so severe?
Poor little Nora, I understand ... you can't believe I've

forgiven you. But I have, Nora. I promise you I have. I've
forgiven you everything. Whatever you did, I know it was
love for me that made you do it.

NORA: That's true.

HELMER: You've loved me as a wife ought to love her husband.
It's just you didn't have the understanding to be able to
judge how you should express it. You mustn't think you're
any less precious to me just because you don't know how to
take the initiative. No, all you have to do is rely on me. I'll
advise you, I'll show you what to do. I wouldn't be a man if
your feminine vulnerability didn't make you doubly
attractive to me. You mustn't take any notice of the hard
things I said, it was just the shock, I was terrified everything
was going to collapse around my ears. I've forgiven you,
Nora. I promise I've forgiven you.

NORA: Thank you for forgiving me.
(*She goes out, right.*)

HELMER: No, just a minute . . . (*Looks through the doorway.*)
What are you doing there?

NORA: (*Offstage*) Taking off my costume.

HELMER: (*In the doorway*) Yes, do. Poor little frightened
songbird, time to calm down now and get back on an even
keel. Rest assured, my wings are broad enough to shelter
you. (*Paces up and down near the door.*) How lovely and
secure our home is, Nora. A sanctuary for you. I'll keep you
here like a hunted dove I've rescued unhurt from the hawk's
talons. I'll calm your poor little pounding heart. Gradually,
Nora. But believe me, by tomorrow everything will look
quite different. And soon things will be just as they were
before. I won't have to keep on saying I've forgiven you.
You'll feel it yourself, unmistakably. How could you
possibly think I'd be capable of disowning you, or even
blaming you for anything? You don't know how generous a
real man can be, Nora. For a man there's something
intensely reassuring and pleasurable about *knowing* that he's
forgiven his wife – and that he's forgiven her sincerely, with
all his heart. It's as if she becomes somehow doubly his

168

possession, as if he's allowed her to be reborn, so that in some way she becomes both his wife and his child. And from now on, that's what you're going to be for me, you confused, helpless little creature. You're not to worry about anything, Nora. Just trust me and I'll be your willpower and your conscience . . . What's going on? Aren't you going to bed? You've changed.

NORA: (*Wearing her everyday dress*) Yes, Torvald, I've changed.

HELMER: But why? I mean it's so late . . .

NORA: I shan't sleep tonight.

HELMER: But, Nora, my dear . . .

NORA: (*Looking at her watch*) It's not that late. Sit down, Torvald. You and I have a lot to talk about.
(*She sits on one side of the table.*)

HELMER: Nora . . . what's the matter? You look so severe . . .

NORA: Sit down. This is going to take some time. I have a lot of things to say to you.
(HELMER *sits opposite her, on the other side of the table.*)

HELMER: You worry me, Nora. I don't understand you.

NORA: No, that's just it. You don't understand me. And I never understood you . . . until this evening. No, you're not to interrupt me. Just listen to what I have to say . . . This is a reckoning, Torvald.

HELMER: What do you mean?

NORA: (*After a short silence*) Does anything strike you about the way we're sitting here now?

HELMER: No, what?

NORA: We've been married now for eight years. Don't you think it's significant that this is the first time you and I as husband and wife have sat down to have a serious talk?

HELMER: What do you mean, serious?

NORA: For eight whole years . . . no, longer than that, from the time we first knew each other, we've never exchanged one serious word on a serious subject.

HELMER: Do you think I should have continually bothered you with all sorts of problems you couldn't possibly have helped me to cope with?

NORA: I'm not talking about your problems. What I'm saying is that we've never sat down and talked and tried to get to the bottom of anything together.

HELMER: But, Nora dear, what good would it do you if we did?

NORA: That's exactly what I mean. You've never understood me. I've been treated very unjustly, Torvald. First by Daddy, and then by you.

HELMER: What do you mean? The two of us have loved you more than anyone else in the world.

NORA: (*Shaking her head*) You've never loved me. You just enjoyed being in love with me.

HELMER: Nora, what is all this?

NORA: It's true, Torvald. When I lived at home with Daddy, he fed me all his opinions, until they became my opinions. Or if they didn't, I kept quiet about it, because I knew he wouldn't have liked it. He used to call me his doll-child and he played with me the way I used to play with my dolls. And when I moved into your house . . .

HELMER: That's no way to describe our marriage.

NORA: (*Unperturbed*) All right, when Daddy handed me over to you. You arranged everything according to your taste and I adapted my taste to yours. Or perhaps I only pretended to, I don't know. Probably a mixture of both, sometimes one, sometimes the other. Now, looking back, I feel as if I've lived a beggar's life – from hand to mouth. I've made my living doing tricks for you, Torvald. And that's what you wanted. You and Daddy have done me great harm. It's your fault I've never come to anything.

HELMER: Nora, how can you be so unreasonable and ungrateful? You've been happy here, haven't you?

NORA: No, never. I thought I was. But I never have been.

HELMER: Not . . . happy!

NORA: No. Cheerful, that's all. You've always been very kind to me. But our house has never been anything but a playroom. I've been your doll-wife, just as I was Daddy's doll-child when I was at home. My children as well, they've been my dolls. I used to enjoy it when you played games with me, just

170

as they enjoyed it when I played games with them. That's all our marriage has been, Torvald.

HELMER: There's some truth in what you say, however exaggerated and hysterical it may be. But from now on all that's going to change. Playtime is over; now it's time you were educated.

NORA: Who? Me or the children?

HELMER: You *and* the children, Nora, my love.

NORA: Oh, Torvald, you're not the man to teach me how to be the right wife for you.

HELMER: How can you say that?

NORA: And as for me . . . what makes me qualified to bring up children?

HELMER: Nora!

NORA: After all, you said it yourself just now – you said you couldn't take the risk.

HELMER: That was in the heat of the moment! You mustn't take any notice of that.

NORA: No, what you said was quite right. I'm not qualified. There's something I have to achieve first. I have to educate myself. And you're not the man to help me with that. I have to do it by myself. That's why I'm leaving you.

HELMER: (*Jumping to his feet*) What did you say?

NORA: I must stand on my own two feet, if I'm to understand myself and the things that are going on around me. That's why I can't stay in your house any longer.

HELMER: Nora, Nora!

NORA: I'm leaving right away. Kristine will put me up for the night . . .

HELMER: Are you mad? You'll do no such thing! I forbid you to!

NORA: It's no use you forbidding me to do anything now. I'll take what belongs to me. I don't want anything from you, now or ever.

HELMER: But this is madness!

NORA: I'm going home tomorrow . . . I mean, back to my old home. It'll be easier for me to find something to do there.

HELMER: It's only lack of experience that makes you so blind . . .

NORA: Experience is something I have to find, Torvald.

HELMER: You can't abandon your home, your husband and your children! What do you think people will say?

NORA: I can't go worrying about that. All I know is that it's something I have to do.

HELMER: But this is outrageous. It's going back on your most sacred duties.

NORA: And what in your opinion are my most sacred duties?

HELMER: Surely you don't have to ask me that. I mean your duties to your husband and your children.

NORA: I have other duties which are just as sacred.

HELMER: No, you haven't. What, for example?

NORA: My duties to myself.

HELMER: Before anything else, you're a wife and a mother.

NORA: I don't believe that any more. I believe that before anything else, I'm a human being, just as much of one as you are . . . or at least I'm going to try to turn myself into one. I know most people would say you were right, Torvald, and I know you'd be backed up by all sorts of books. But what most people say and what you find in books just doesn't satisfy me any more. I want to think everything out for myself and make my own decisions.

HELMER: You don't seem to understand your position in your own home. There's an infallible guide in this sort of situation, you know. There's your religion, what about that?

NORA: Oh, Torvald, I really don't know what religion is.

HELMER: What are you trying to say?

NORA: All I know is what Pastor Hansen told me, when I was confirmed. He told me religion was this, religion was that. When I've got out of all this and I'm on my own, I'll be able to think the whole thing over. I want to see whether the things Pastor Hansen told me are true, or at any rate whether they're true for me.

HELMER: But that kind of thing is unheard of for a young woman! Well, if you refuse to be guided by your religion, at least let me appeal to your conscience. I suppose you do have some sort of moral code? Or perhaps you don't? Mm?

NORA: Well, Torvald, it's not a very easy question to answer. I really don't know. I find it all quite bewildering. The only thing I do know is that my opinions about these things are quite different from yours. I've also found out that the law is different from what I thought. What I can't accept is that the law is right. That a woman shouldn't be allowed to avoid hurting her old, dying father or save her husband's life. I won't accept that.

HELMER: Don't be so childish. You don't understand the first thing about the society you're living in.

NORA: No, I don't. That's why I want to make myself part of it. Then I'll be able to make up my mind which of us is right – society or me.

HELMER: I think you must be ill, Nora. Feverish. You seem to have lost your senses.

NORA: I've never felt as convinced and as lucid as I am tonight.

HELMER: You're convinced and lucid and you're abandoning your husband and children . . .

NORA: Yes. That's right.

HELMER: Then there's only one possible explanation.

NORA: What's that?

HELMER: You don't love me any more.

NORA: That's exactly it.

HELMER: Nora! . . . How can you say that?

NORA: It hurts me very much to say it, Torvald, you've always been so kind to me. But there's nothing I can do about it. I don't love you any more.

HELMER: (*Making an effort to be calm*) And you've thought about this and you're quite sure?

NORA: Absolutely positive. That's why I don't want to stay here any more.

HELMER: Can you explain to me why it is I've lost your love?

NORA: Yes, I can. It was this evening, when the miracle didn't happen. That's when I realized you weren't the man I thought you were.

HELMER: Can't you be a bit more explicit? I don't understand.

NORA: I've waited so patiently, eight years now. God, I knew well enough you can't expect miracles to happen every day. But when this terrible storm broke over me, I was sure it couldn't fail to come: the miracle. While Krogstad's letter was lying out there, it never occurred to me for a minute that you could possibly give in to his conditions. I was sure you were bound to say, tell the whole world if you want to. And once that had happened . . .

HELMER: You mean you think I should have let my own wife be exposed to shame and disgrace . . . ?

NORA: Once that had happened, I was sure you were bound to step forward and take all the blame yourself and say, I'm the guilty one.

HELMER: Nora . . . !

NORA: You mean I would never have let you make a sacrifice like that? No, of course I wouldn't. But what could I have done? It would have been my word against yours . . . *That* was the miracle I was hoping for in my misery. And it was to prevent *that* that I wanted to kill myself.

HELMER: I'd gladly work day and night for you, Nora . . . put up with any suffering or hardship for your sake. But no one would sacrifice his honour, even for love.

NORA: Millions of women have.

HELMER: You think and talk like an ignorant child.

NORA: Maybe. But you don't think or talk like the man I want to spend my life with. When you stopped being terrified – not about what threatened me, but about your own reputation – once you had nothing more to fear, then, as far as you were concerned, it was as if the whole thing had never happened. Everything was exactly as before, I was your little lark, your doll, from now on you'd be doubly careful looking after me, because I was so frail and delicate . . . (*Stands up.*) At that moment, Torvald, I realized that I'd been living with a stranger for eight years and that I'd had three children by him . . . I can't bear to think about it! I could tear myself to pieces.

HELMER: (*Sadly*) I see. I see. A chasm has opened up between us . . . Isn't . . . isn't there any way we could bridge it, Nora?

NORA: The way I am now, I'm no sort of a wife for you.

HELMER: I'm strong enough to change.

NORA: Perhaps . . . if your doll is taken away from you.

HELMER: To be separated . . . separated from you. No, Nora, I
    just can't grasp the idea.

NORA: (*Going into the room on the right*) All the more reason for it to
    happen.
    (*She comes back with her overcoat and a small overnight bag
    which she puts on a chair by the table.*)

HELMER: Not now, Nora, please. Wait until tomorrow.

NORA: (*Putting on her coat*) I can't stay the night in a stranger's
    house.

HELMER: But can't we live here as brother and sister . . . ?

NORA: (*Tying on her hat*) You know very well that couldn't last
    long . . . (*Wraps her shawl around her.*) Goodbye, Torvald. I
    don't want to see the children. I know they're in better hands
    than mine. The way I am now, I'd be no use to them.

HELMER: But some time, Nora . . . later . . . ?

NORA: How can I tell? I've no idea what's going to become of me.

HELMER: But you're my wife, you are now and you always will be.

NORA: Listen, Torvald . . . when a wife leaves her husband, as I am
    leaving you now, as far as I understand it, legally he's absolved
    from all obligations towards her. In any case, *I'm* releasing
    you from all your obligations. You mustn't feel restricted in
    any way, I'm not going to. Complete freedom on both sides.
    Look, here's your ring back. Give me mine.

HELMER: That as well?

NORA: That as well.

HELMER: Here you are.

NORA: Right. Now it's all over. Here are the keys. The servants
    know everything about the house . . . more than I do, really.
    I'll be setting off tomorrow and I'll send Kristine round to
    pack up the things I brought with me from home. I want them
    sent on to me.

HELMER: All over, all over. Nora, won't you ever think of me again?

NORA: Of course I'll think of you and the children and the house,
    often.

HELMER: May I write to you, Nora?

NORA: No, never. Don't.

HELMER: But can't I send you . . . ?

NORA: Nothing. Nothing.

HELMER: . . .or help you, if you need it?

NORA: No, I've told you. I don't accept anything from strangers.

HELMER: Nora . . . can't I ever be anything but a stranger to you?

NORA: (*Picking up her overnight bag*) Oh, Torvald, there would have to be the most wonderful miracle . . .

HELMER: What sort of miracle, tell me!

NORA: Both of us would change so much that . . . Oh, Torvald, I don't believe in miracles any more.

HELMER: But I'll believe in it. Tell me! We'd have to change so much that . . .

NORA: That our life together would become a marriage. Goodbye.
(*She goes into the hall.* HELMER *sinks into a chair by the door and buries his face in his hands.*)

HELMER: Nora! Nora! (*Looks around and gets up.*) Empty. She's gone. (*Hope rising in him.*) The most wonderful miracle . . .
(*From below, the heavy sound of a door closing.*)

6/12/93